# Meditation – The Royal Road to the Soul

Niels Brønsted

# MEDITATION

## The Royal Road to the Soul

FSC
www.fsc.org
MIX
Papir fra
ansvarlige kilder
Paper from
responsible sources
FSC® C105338


Danish title: *Meditation – Kongevejen til sjælen*
Translated into English by Paul Birkholm and Niels Brønsted
Cover illustration: Britta Brønsted
Editing: Michael von Bülow

Publisher: BoD – Books on Demand, Hellerup, Denmark
Printing: BoD – Books on Demand, Norderstedt, Germany

Second Edition in English 2024
ISBN 978-87-43057-82-6

# Content

Page

Foreword ........ 1
Introduction ........ 3
Esoteric Man ........ 8
The "Self" or "I" ........ 13
  The Dimensions of the Self ........ 17
  Illumination ........ 18
Qualities ........ 22
  Aspiration ........ 22
  Perseverance ........ 24
  Concentration ........ 25
  The Mind – an Independent Being ........ 28
  Visualization ........ 30
Meditation ........ 33
  Alignment ........ 34
  Dedication ........ 37
  Meditation ........ 38
  Meditation with Seed Thought ........ 39
  Meditation without Seed Thought ........ 45
  Creative Meditation ........ 52
  The Method of Meditation ........ 55
  Contemplation ........ 57
  Illumination ........ 59
  Realization and Service ........ 61
Invocation and Evocation ........ 62
The Creative Word ........ 64
The Practical Work ........ 70
  Place ........ 70
  Time ........ 71
  Rhythm ........ 72
  Posture ........ 72
  Breath ........ 73
Evening Review ........ 74
  The Review Itself ........ 76

Group Meditation .......... 81
Introduction .......... 81
Group Consciousness .......... 84
Group Meditation .......... 87
Full Moon Meditation .......... 93
Elements of Danger .......... 101
Dangers Inherent in the Personality .......... 104
Dangers Arising from Karma and Surroundings .......... 107
Dangers from Beings on the Inner Planes .......... 109
Conclusion .......... 111
The Great Invocation .......... 114
Bibliography .......... 115
Esoteric Literature for "Beginners" .......... 116

## Meditations

Meditation – Disidentification .......... 15
Exercise in Concentration .......... 30
Exercise in Visualization .......... 32
Meditation – Alignment .......... 36
Meditation with Seed Thought .......... 43
Meditation without Seed Thought .......... 50
Creative Meditation .......... 54
Occult Meditation .......... 66
Evening Review .......... 79
Group Meditation .......... 90
Full Moon Meditation .......... 96

## Illustrations

Figure 1 – The Planes and the Structure of Man .......... 9
Figure 2 – The Bodies of Man .......... 11
Figure 3 – The Carriage – drawing by Britta Brønsted .......... 14
Figure 4 – Map of Consciousness .......... 19
Figure 5 – Meditation – Ascent and Descent .......... 35

# Foreword

The concept of meditation has been known all over the world for many years, and today there are plenty of inviting offers to active and potential "consumers". But at the same time, meditation is an integral part of the modern esoteric teaching, as it is expressed in sources like classical theosophical literature and the works of Alice A. Bailey, Lucille Cedercrans, and others.

In this context, the concept of meditation is somewhat narrowed down, because here are certain requirements as to the intention and motivation behind the meditation work. That is why this form of activity is often termed "occult meditation". The word "occult" means something like "concealed", and when it is used in combination with meditation it is implied that this activity is aiming at revealing hidden or latent qualities in a human being – that is, the inherent ability in all individuals to develop conscious contact with their own souls.

But not many people are aware of this aspect of meditation, and that may be due to the fact that there are not so many books in the world focusing on that aspect. That is why I have written this book. My primary intention is to inspire as many people as possible to make meditation part of their everyday life pattern. If they have a natural affinity to modern esotericism,[1] this book may give them the rationale of meditation. If they are unfamiliar with esoteric words and concepts they merely have to accept that scattered throughout the book will be pages and passages which may not be easily understandable. But this does not in any way prevent them from learning to meditate, for all the necessary information is easily accessible.

One of the consequences of the close connection between meditation and the esoteric teaching is that a book of this type necessarily has certain limitations. It is not possible to develop the meditation work beyond a certain limit without a closer study of the laws and principles governing the processes and expansions of consciousness, which are the natural outcome of prolonged exercise of the esoteric form of meditation. These studies will lead the practitioner toward far more advanced forms of meditation, which are entirely

[1] *Esotericism*: Concerning the esoteric teaching.

beyond the scope of this book, and which it would be futile to describe.

These aspects of meditation are hinted at in the last chapter of the book – the Conclusion – where I suggest a way of dealing with the inherent limitations of the book.

But before we begin our study of meditation, I want to point out that I have chosen Michal Eastcott's book *The Silent Path*[1] as my structural starting point, and even if the present book is entirely different in its final presentation I want to acknowledge the kinship with the above work, which, in my opinion, still is a unique contribution to the literature about meditation. At the same time, I thank The Sundial House Group for permission to quote from the mentioned book, and Lucis Trust and Wisdom Impressions for granting me a general permission to use the works of Alice A. Bailey and Lucille Cedercrans, respectively, in my esoteric work.

[1] Rider 1969.

# Introduction

Michal Eastcott begins her book by quoting the English journalist and writer Paul Brunton. He says, "We do not hear the sun rise"– even if it is the most essential event in nature. "So too, the greatest moments in a man's life come quietly".[1] This image, Michael Eastcott expands in a very poetic and at the same time extremely realistic way:

> *"The path of meditation can well be compared with the long stillness before day-break. There is frequently nothing to mark it but a quietly increasing light. The gradual dawning of a new world in our consciousness comes silently. It is a secret, inner thing which we can never fully share with others"...*[2]

In this stillness, we may contact inner dimensions of consciousness which are not normally at the disposal of our physical consciousness. But we do not doubt for a minute that they exist, for we have all tried to drift about in the realms of the imagination and seen how real they are.

These are what much literature and poetry are about, and their reality are confirmed by our dreams. When we wake up after a night's sleep we often have the impression that we have been somewhere else, and that we brought all of our "person" with us – except for the physical body, of course.

In the East, it has been known for thousands of years that meditation is a way of contacting the inner dimensions. In the West, we have not really known meditation. The closest we get is probably prayer or religious reflection while walking about in fragrant flower gardens, reading the books of the mystics.

That meditation has been known in the East is due to the fact that this activity really is an integral part of a spiritual teaching which has been present in that part of the world for thousands of years. We find it in Hinduism, Taoism, and later also in Buddhism.

[1] Michael Eastcott: *The Silent Path*, p. 3.

[2] *Ibid.*, p. 3.

But in the East, the teaching had only very little social effect. As in the West, there has always been enormous differences between rich and poor people, but in the East the situation even developed so far as to allow people to die in the streets before the very eyes of their fellow beings, and that rarely happens among the populations of the West.

Naturally, this is a controversial statement, so let us see what one of the absolute key figures of the esoteric teaching has to say about this question. It is the Tibetan Master Djwhal Khul, D.K. or just "the Tibetan" who employed the English esotericist and writer Alice A. Bailey as his secretary or amanuensis. Her influence today is so wide-spread that many esotericists all over the world consider her "blue" books as the most comprehensive and profound spiritual impulse humanity has ever received. She (or maybe we should say he) makes the following statement:

> *"The East has had this teaching for ages and has produced numerous commentaries upon it – the work of the finest analytical minds that the world has ever seen – but it has made no mass use of the knowledge, and the people in the Orient do not profit by it, as a whole. It will be different in the West and is already modifying and influencing human thought on a large scale; it is permeating the structure of our civilisation and will eventually salvage it".*[1]

The spiritual teaching is made available for humanity by those individuals who have passed through the path of human evolution before us, and who therefore call themselves our "elder brothers." They are "Masters", in the same way as a carpenter or a mason becomes a master when he masters his profession. They have solved all human problems, they master everything which is human, and they are now in the possession of the collective repertoire of perfected human qualities.

Some of these qualities are lying dormant in our spiritual nature for millions of years and do not surface until we, on our own initiative, are making a conscious effort to unfold them. But that this

[1] Alice A. Bailey: *Esoteric Psychology II,* p. 511.

is at all possible to do in a relatively concentrated manner, within a span of time which is far shorter than that nature would have spent if it were left to itself, is due to the fact that some of these Masters have been kind enough to tell us how they made it themselves. This is really one of the core concepts of the esoteric teaching, and it is beautifully expressed by the Tibetan:

> *"He who faces the light and stands within its radiance is blinded to the issues of the world of men; he passes on the lighted way to the great Centre of Absorption. But he who feels the urge to pass that way, yet loves his brother on the darkened path, revolves upon the pedestal of light and turns the other way. He faces towards the dark and then the seven points of light within himself transmit the outward streaming light, and lo! the face of those upon the darkened way receives that light. For them, the way is not so dark"...*[1]

That the teaching comes from the Masters implies that its primary purpose is to "persuade" or "manipulate" people to transform themselves and the society they live in, for those Masters serve the whole of humanity and not just a "selected" band of pilgrims. That is why, in their eyes, it is disastrous when the teaching does not have noticeable social effects, for it means that it is merely perceived theoretically and does not result in the unfoldment of that love and wisdom which is the inevitable outcome, when its message is transformed into practical usefulness and compassionate service by those who study it.

Therefore, at some appropriate time, the Spiritual Hierarchy[2] of our world decided to move the focal point of the spiritual teaching from the East to the West where it finds today expression in the modern scientific, esoteric teaching – scientific because it is empirical, that is, based on experience.

The peoples of the West have a somewhat different psychological profile compared to that of the eastern populations. We are pri-

[1] Alice A. Bailey: *Discipleship in the New Age II*, p. 15.

[2] *The Hierarchy*: The group of Masters that is present on earth as responsible for the planetary evolution and is therefore, by some, called "The Inner Government of the World".

marily characterized by the psychological aspect which esoterically is called "active intelligence", while the peoples of the East are more inward-looking and known for their intuitive wisdom.

But the transference of the focus of the spiritual teaching also means that meditation is rapidly becoming part of Western culture. And according to our psychological profile, we have started right away to seek for our inner sources by the aid of meditation– carried out with scientific precision and care. When this happens in the life and evolution of individual man is specified clearly by the Tibetan, for he says:

> *"As long as the polarisation is purely physical or purely emotional, no need for meditation is ever felt. Even when the mental body is active, no urge arises until the man has run through many changes and many lives, has tasted the cup of pleasure and of pain through many incarnations, has sounded the depths of the life lived entirely for the lower self and found it unsatisfying. Then he begins to turn his thought to other things, to aspire to that which is unknown, to realize and sense within himself the pairs of opposites, and to contact within his consciousness possibilities and ideals undreamt of hitherto. He has come to a point where success, popularity and diverse gifts are his, and yet from their use he derives no content; always the urge within persists until the pain is so severe that the desire to reach out and up, to ascertain something and someone beyond, overcomes all obstacles. The man begins to turn within and to seek the source from whence he came. Then he begins to meditate, to ponder, to intensify vibration until in process of time he garners the fruits of meditation".*[1]

That the teaching has its primary focal point in the West also means that it will be disseminated to a far higher degree than it was in the East. Today, by way of the Internet, we may order any book which is not out of print – including esoteric books.

Moreover, we see that the "thought climate" which the esoteric teaching has been establishing during the last 125 years, combined with the impulse of Christianity, is gradually beginning to influence

[1] Alice A. Bailey: *Letters on Occult Meditation*, pp. 9-10.

the social functions of society. A social legislation as for instance that of Denmark is a clear expression of that process, for it has involved a political majority which has "voted" it into our system. This implies a certain degree of sympathy and compassion for the weakest in society – the poor, the diseased, and the unemployed – who have greater difficulty in supporting themselves than other people. They are certainly not allowed to die in the streets.

# Esoteric Man

The esoteric teaching tells us that there are other dimensions of substance than the physical – which most people still believe to be the only one. It also tells us that man is a spiritual being who incarnates in those dimensions in order to develop his potential. Fundamentally, he is a "spark" or "quantum" of pure life energy which is esoterically termed a "monad",[1] and when this energy is anchored in substance or matter a third factor arises – a factor called "consciousness". We see a parallel to that phenomenon in the fact that when en electric current passes through a wire it develops a magnetic field around the wire.

This means that man incarnates in order to develop consciousness, but it takes a long series of lives or incarnations to reach the final stage we have previously described as "Master". So, the esoteric teaching claims that there is an evolution on earth but that it is primarily an evolution of consciousness and only secondarily a form evolution.

The dimensions of substance into which the monads incarnate are also termed "worlds" or "planes". Each plane is an energy field with a definite range of frequencies representing definite types of consciousness. There are 7 of these planes, and during their evolution human beings have developed a "body" or "vehicle" in the 3 "lowest" dimensions – that is, those with the lowest frequencies. This is best illustrated by a drawing – Figure 1.

So, the bodies are organs in which the soul develops consciousness, and the body which is the most advanced in its evolution is the double physical vehicle consisting of a biological cell body and a so-called "etheric" or "vital" body. This is in the nature of an energy field which permeates the dense body and stretches a few centimetres outside of it.

At his present level of evolution, man is fully conscious in the dimension of the dense physical body and has the ability to perceive his surroundings in a clear and concise way. This physical awareness we may term the "outer" or "objective" part of our consciousness, because it is anchored in the brain and nervous systems and is measurable by electrodes.

[1] *Monad*: Greek, "unity".

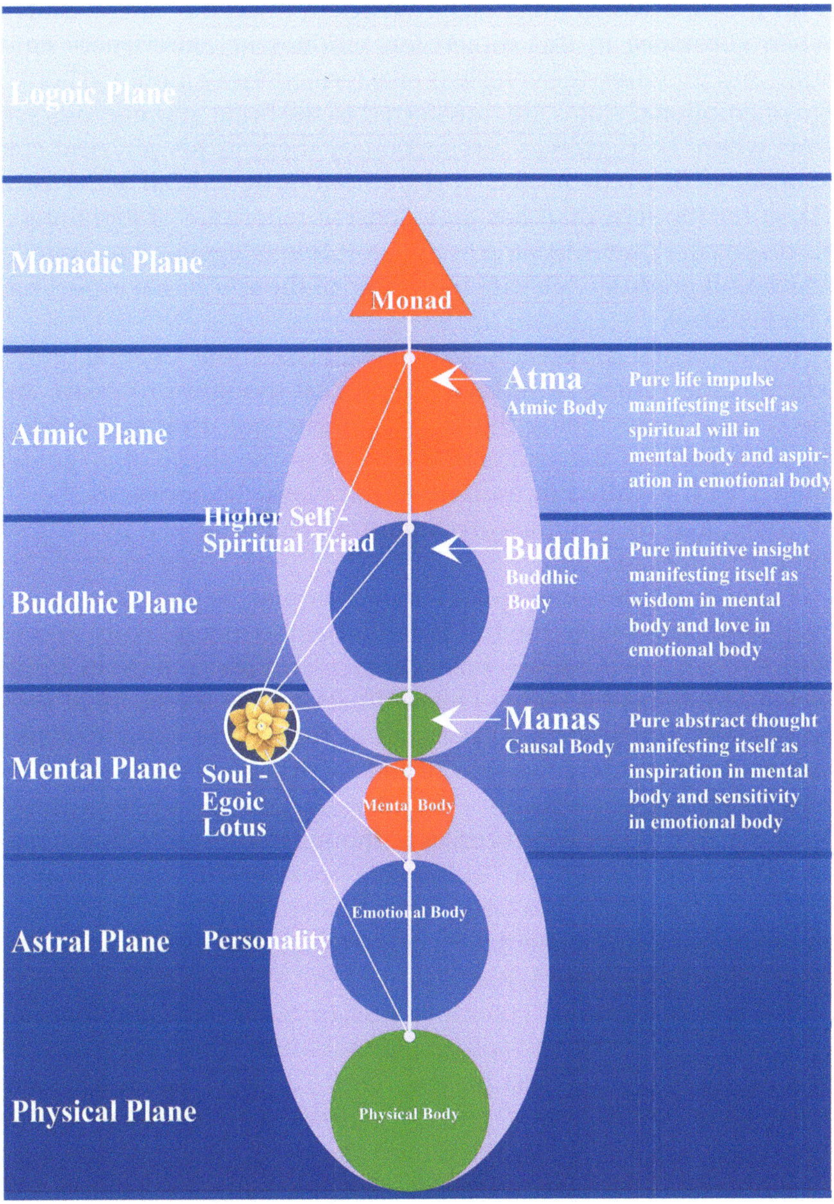
Logoic Plane
Monadic Plane
Monad
Atmic Plane
Atma
Atmic Body
Pure life impulse manifesting itself as spiritual will in mental body and aspiration in emotional body
Higher Self - Spiritual Triad
Buddhic Plane
Buddhi
Buddhic Body
Pure intuitive insight manifesting itself as wisdom in mental body and love in emotional body
Mental Plane
Soul - Egoic Lotus
Manas
Causal Body
Pure abstract thought manifesting itself as inspiration in mental body and sensitivity in emotional body
Mental Body
Astral Plane
Personality
Emotional Body
Physical Plane
Physical Body

Figure 1

In the next world, man has a vehicle termed the "astral body". When substance in this dimension vibrates he experiences emotions, and therefore the vehicle is also termed the "emotional body". These emotional states are transferred to the brain and nervous systems where he perceives a reflection of them in his physical consciousness. But in their own world, emotions include all of the astral plane, for modern man has an extensive repertoire of emotions at his disposal. What is lacking in his evolution is a general refinement which will gradually elevate the whole of the emotional aspect into a higher level.

In the mental dimension, man has 2 bodies: the "mental body", which is the vehicle of ordinary analytical thought processes, and the "causal body" being the vehicle of the soul itself and holding the focal point of the soul consciousness in the shape of a "golden lotus",[1] as it is called in esoteric terminology. It represents the "I" or "self", and its activities are first of all characterized by abstract thinking, love, and will.

The mental development of man has just begun. Only a few people – if any – have the full potential of the mental body at their disposal, while even fewer have contact with the soul in the upper region of the mental plane. This is illustrated by the fact that most people only use some 5-10 per cent of their brain capacity which reflects the thought processes of the mental body in the physical consciousness.

These two types of processes – thoughts and emotions – may be termed the "inner" or "subjective" part of our consciousness, because it cannot be measured but only experienced. The physical, emotional, and lower mental aspects together are usually called the personality (see Figure 1, p. 9).

The higher regions of consciousness, from the buddhic plane and upwards, represent latent spiritual possibilities which at present are beyond the range of most people. They can only be brought into being when we initiate a process of systematic spiritual unfoldment, as it is described by the esoteric teaching. Then we develop a buddhic and atmic body as vehicles for spiritual intuition and will,

[1] *Golden lotus*: See cover illustration.

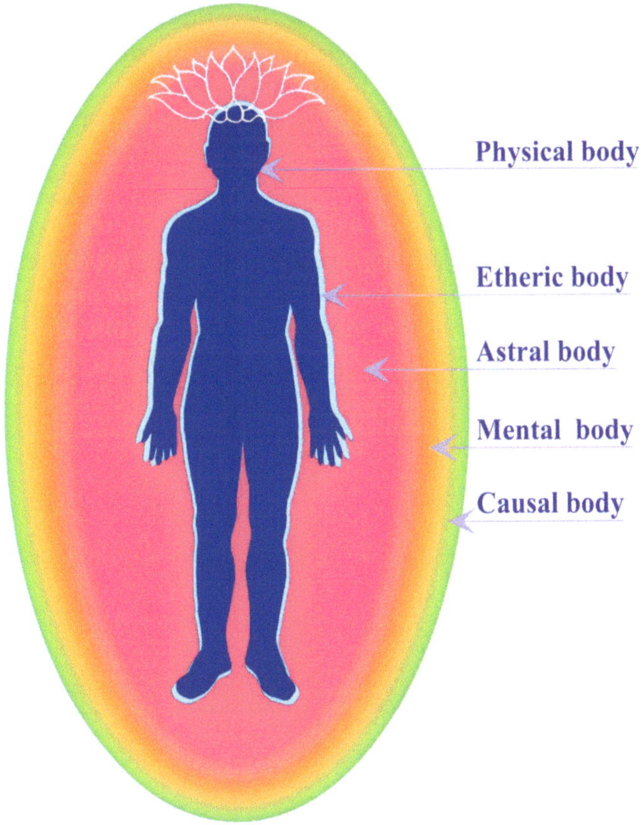


Figure 2

respectively, and together with the causal body they manifest the higher self (see Figure 1).

But as this phase of evolution lies ahead of most people, we are able to depict man's total esoteric structure as shown on Figure 2.[1] Here we see that our bodies are not piled on top of each other – as might be inferred from Figure 1 – but interpenetrate the dense physical body and stretching beyond. The higher the frequency of a body the greater its extension, and at the same time it pervades the other vehicles without interfering with their processes of consciousness.

[1] The colours shown are merely illustrative and in no way represent the real appearance of the bodies (this note applies to colour print versions of the book only).

It may be disappointing to some people that what is normally called "spiritual development" is in the future for them, but here it is wise to remember that the term "spiritual development" is very wide, and that all development is really "spiritual." The Tibetan says:

> *"It could be proved that the word "spiritual" covered every phase of living experience… That is spiritual which lies beyond the point of present achievement; it is that which embodies the vision and which urges the man on towards a goal higher than the one attained".*[1]

[1] Alice A. Bailey: *Discipleship in the New Age II*, p. 234.

# The "Self" or "I"

As we can see on Figure 1, page 9, the evolution of man consists in developing consciousness in the "higher" mental and spiritual spheres and connecting these states with those of the personality so that they may be expressed in family life and the social relations of society.

But if we want to understand this process of evolution, we should be aware of the fact that there is a common denominator for all processes of consciousness – whether they are inner and psychical[1] or outer and physical. This is the "self" or "I" who is behind and participates in these processes.

We may not always be aware of that because we tend to identify with the processes of the bodies and think we *are* our thoughts, emotions, and actions. If we observe ourselves, we are often surprised to see how many currents our consciousness really consist of. Different parts of our being sort of live their own lives and may even oppose each other. One part may be afraid, while another tries to calm that emotion, one part is over-active, while another is tired and lazy, one part is rebellious, and another quiet and accepting.

But an observation of these processes helps us to distinguish between the self and the various states of consciousness, for these do not represent the "self" or "I" and hardly influence it. The currents come and go, but if we look back at ourselves through a longer period of time, we will find that there is a permanent core which is unchangeable all through life. Maybe the best expression is "pure being".

It means that we do not really get older, and that the statement made by our parents thousands of times, that we would some day "grow up", never really happens as a specific incident. This may be wise to keep in mind for youngsters when they associate with older people. We may be slower, more rheumatic and crystallized in outer appearance, but inside we are not older than other people. We may still spin like a top on the pavement when we see a beautiful woman or man.

[1] *Psychical*: Of the soul or mind. *Psukhe* is Greek for soul.

Figure 3

But what is the self then, we might ask? There is an old Eastern image which is a very good illustration – see Figure 3:

The carriage is the physical body, the horses are the emotional nature, the driver is the intellect, while the passenger in the carriage is the self or soul. He makes decisions pertaining to all of the vehicle – where it is going and when – while the driver just steers the carriage and manages the horses.

But the best impression of the differences between the self and its functions or processes we may get from a meditation. The technical background for this meditation is found in the book *Psychosynthesis* by Roberto Assagioli,[1] but in its present form it is edited and expanded so that it serves esoteric more than therapeutic purposes. During the meditation, we will simply see if we can meet the self face to face – however briefly it may be.

[1] Reprinted in Psychosynthesis Practice, Vol. 1, p. 11.

## Meditation – Disidentification

Sit comfortably, relax your body completely, straighten your back, and close your eyes. Rest your hands and arms in a natural manner, and keep your feet firmly anchored on the floor. Take a deep breath, and then forget all about the breath.

The meditation consists of a few sentences you say in your mind. In between the sentences, you think about their meaning, and here the commentaries after every sentence may serve as guiding lines.

Say in your mind:
*I have a body, but I am not this body and its actions – I am the one who acts.*

The body is an instrument, enabling me to move about. It is the seat of my senses, and I use it when I perceive and communicate with my surroundings. I treat it well, I keep it healthy, but I am not this body.

Say in your mind:
*I feel, but I am not my feelings – I am the one who feels.*

I oscillate between pleasure and pain, joy and sorrow, high and low spirits, but my inner being does not change. I may observe these fluctuations and learn to use them for communication, and therefore I cannot be my emotions.

Say in your mind:
*I think, but I am not my thoughts – I am the one who thinks.*

Thought assists me in observing and understanding my surroundings and myself. It is able to remember my previous experiences, make new experiences, and compare them to each other. But it is not my inner being, for I may decide for myself what I want to think.

Say in your mind:
*I have a personality, but I am not this person – I am the one who is posing.*

I have many activities and play many roles. At home I am one, at work another, and together with strangers a third. But I am aware of it, I can see myself play these roles, so therefore they are not my inner being.

Say in your mind:
*Then, what am I? What is left when I have withdrawn from these functions? There is a centre of pure awareness of self, of pure will.*

But here is an important thing we may learn about this self.

Say in your mind:
*Now I have observed the body, emotions, thoughts, and the personality. But who is observing the observer, the self? No one does that.*

We cannot see the self, like we cannot see the sun but only its radiation. We merely see the activities of the self, and when they die down only the self is left. It takes up all of the silver screen of the mind so that there is nothing else but the self. Therefore, it cannot be my self contrary to the self of others. It is the same all-embracing self in all people, and my individual self stands in relation to this All-self as the drop to the ocean.

Say in your mind:
*The self is the same in all people. There is only one self. I am that self, that self am I.*

## The Dimensions of the Self

The meditation showed us that the self or "I" is experienced as a vacuum which is left when all the processes of consciousness die down – even if it is only for a brief moment. But the fact that it is a vacuum, that there is only one factor in the field of consciousness, indicates that the self is not personal, for otherwise there would have been 2 factors: our self and the surroundings.

Nevertheless, we usually perceive our self to be something which constitutes us personally. So, if at the same time it is the self of everybody else, there must be deeper layers which we are unable to experience directly in physical consciousness. The conception of a personal self must be a projection of something far deeper in our nature. This, another great esotericist has commented on, namely, Lucille Cedercrans who worked as a secretary for the Hungarian Master Rakoczy, in exactly the same manner as Alice A. Bailey worked with the Tibetan. Naturally, in both cases, it is an entirely voluntary co-operation of great benefit to the secretaries. She says:

> *"The consciousness which is focused in the brain, which refers to itself as 'I' is an extension or projection, if you wish to call it that, of the Soul itself. That which thinks of itself as 'I', which has identified itself with its instrument, is in truth but an expansion of the spiritual Soul consciousness.*
>
> *It has first to awaken to the fact that there is such a thing as a spiritual Soul; that it has a direct relationship to that spiritual Soul; so that there is a sense of duality created in the identification awareness of the personality consciousness. It identifies the spiritual Soul as its higher self and itself (personality consciousness) as the lower self. In aspiration, then, the personality consciousness seeks to contact the Soul; to become aware of the fact of its existence, not only in theory, but in the realm of experience; to experience via contact the actuality of the Soul.*
>
> *The first objective of the Soul, mind and brain alignment is to provide this experience for the personality consciousness during the present incarnation. That objective is an immediate objective. He knows that the personality consciousness must experience the reality*

*of the Soul via contact, if the theory of the higher consciousness is to be translated into a fact in nature, that it is only such an experience which will provide the personality with sufficient impetus to undergo the necessary disciplines to achieve a final union with that Soul".*[1]

This we may illustrate by a map of our consciousness – see Figure 4[2]. The numbers on the drawing refer to the following aspects of consciousness – briefly enumerated:

1. *The lower unconscious.* Holds the instinctual life which is normally not accessible to the waking consciousness. Generally, it represents the past.
2. *The middle unconscious.* Formed of psychological elements similar to those of the waking consciousness and easily accessible to it. Represents the present.
3. *The higher unconscious or superconscious.* The source of inspirations and intuitions which are normally beyond the reach of the waking consciousness. Represents the future.
4. *The waking consciousness.*
5. *The personal self or "I".*
6. *The Higher self.*
7. *The collective unconscious.*

## Illumination

From the map, we see that it is possible to create a connection between the personal and the higher spiritual self, and the method is meditation. This connection passes through the higher unconscious or superconscious area, and it is precisely the deeper purpose of meditation to bring the aspirant in touch with this area, for it enables him to see ordinary life in another and higher perspective. This is called illumination.

[1] Lucille Cedercrans: *Applied Wisdom – Volume I*, pp. 28-29.

[2] Copyright © Nomina, Rome, Italy. The technical content is derived from Roberto Assagioli's book *Psychosynthesis*, p. 17.

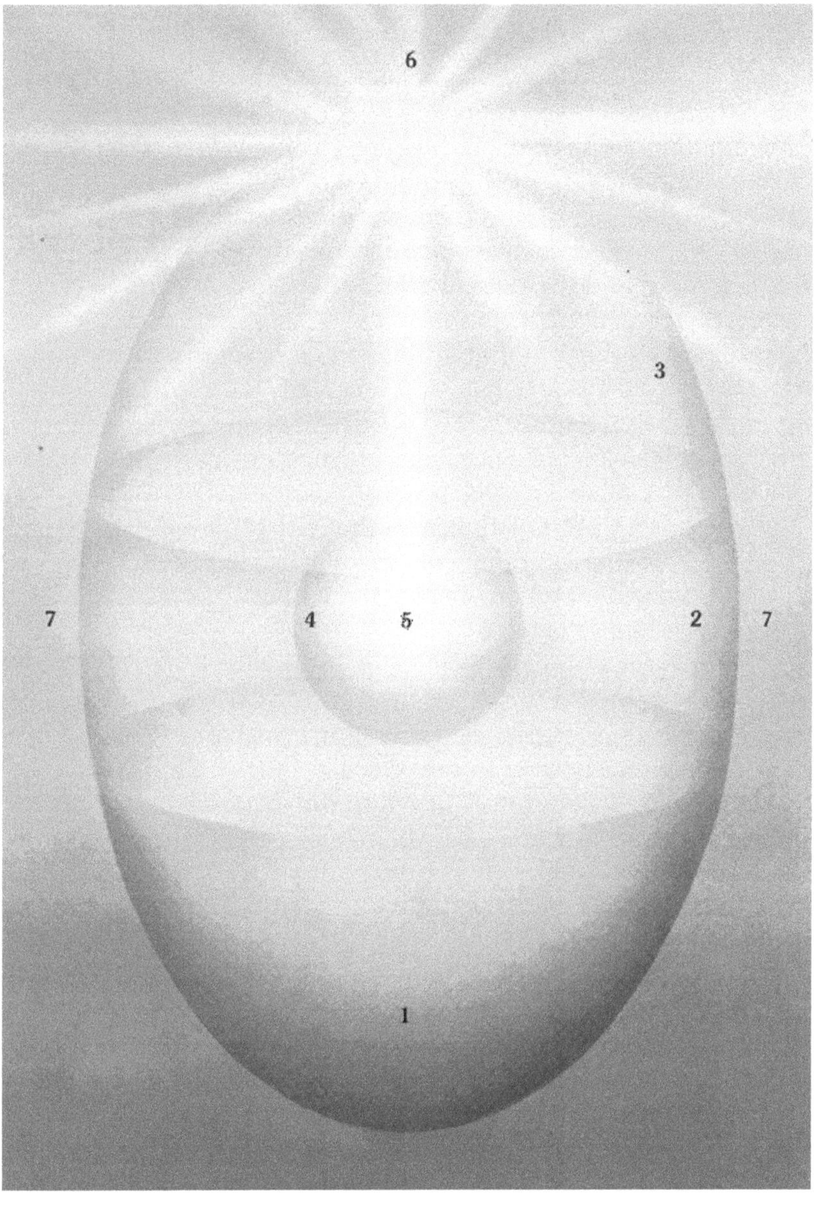


Figure 4

But when we climb a mountain there are several plateaus on the way, and this is also true here. The outlook of the meditating person gets higher and higher, and this means that the experience of illumination has differing stages.

*Illumination in the emotional nature.* People who experience illumination in the region of the emotions are filled with a boundless euphoric well-being, giving them the excess of energy that enables them to be devoted to the surrounding world. The condition is termed ecstasy, and the person who experiences it is often called a "mystic".

But like any other emotional state we like, it causes desire to experience it as often as possible, and when it is there, to maintain it as long as possible. And that which we desire is always something we want for ourselves. We do not feel a burning desire for our neighbor to have a new car.

But naturally, it is not the primary goal of meditation to have a good time and steep ourselves in celestial happiness and well-being. This is evident when we observe what happens when illumination is on a higher level.

*Illumination in the realm of thought.* People who experience illumination in the world of thought are flooded with a light which is lifting the mental function as a whole up to abstract and intuitive levels. Everything is seen in one eternal "now". This does not require a logical procedure of thought, and it raises no questions – what is experienced is real and true.

The condition is termed "contemplation", and the type of process is often called "occult" meditation. Contrary to the process of the mystic, this meditation awakens the urge to bring the experience down into the physical brain consciousness so that it may be realized in service work for humanity.

This is due to the fact that the closer we approach the higher self the closer we approach other people, for we have seen that there is but one self – the same in all people.

In the remaining part of the book we will solely concern ourselves with occult meditation which is the primary technique used on the path of spiritual evolution as it is described today. But at the same time, occult meditation is also the core of the old raja yoga system that Patanjali assembled in his *Yoga Sutras*, and which Alice A. Bailey presented in her book *The Light of the Soul*. The Tibetan gave her the sutras while she herself wrote the commentaries.

Raja yoga means "royal" yoga because it is a method which produces a unification of all 3 primary aspects of a human being – personality, soul, and spirit. Therefore, it is the crowning glory, the highest form of yoga which was developed in India. And naturally, this is the connotation to the word which has given rise to the subtitle of the present book – *The Royal Road to the Soul*.

But before we take a closer look at the process of meditation we should make it plain which qualities are required if we want to start meditating. Naturally, we are not able to cover all aspects of this vast area, but we will mention the primary qualities and leave it to the reader to complete the list.

# Qualities

## Aspiration

If a person wants to start meditating he should have a deep wish to do so, or – as it probably is in most cases – a deep wish to obtain the "effects" meditation is said to have. If there is no such wish it is most unlikely that he will ever be able to muster the perseverance, which is another quality meditation presupposes.

These "effects" of meditation could be termed "spiritual development," and so we may say that the person in question should have a desire for spiritual unfoldment. This is called "aspiration",[1] and the person is called an "aspirant". This expression is used relatively often in this book but should not be taken too literally in the technical esoteric connotation of the word. Usually, the meaning is simply a "seeker". Another word which is also used fairly often is "disciple". This means "pupil", but again it should not be taken too literally in this book, as it is normally used to denote an aspirant on a somewhat higher level of evolution.

Esoterically, the aspirant is a person who has passed the phase which is termed the "culmination" of the personality and has experienced for himself that the satisfaction of desire does not make him happy – which he has believed during the long evolutionary journey up to this point. But he is unable to simply stop desiring, and therefore he starts to desire something else but material welfare and the pleasures of the senses which altogether constitute what we call "materialism".

He has painfully ascertained that the physical world, in which he has been focused so far, does not provide what he is looking for, and therefore he begins to desire some "other reality" which can give him the satisfaction the physical world denies him. In other words, he desires spiritual development in the hope that it will make him happy in another way.

At the same time, he understands that he must make sacrifices in order to reach the "Promised Land" he has heard or read about, for this is an intelligent and strong-willed person, who has been able

[1] *Aspiration*: An earnest desire for something.

to reach the top of his profession and consequently seen for himself that "nothing comes of nothing", that if you want to reach your goal you have to invest and make an effort.

Very often it is this kind of person who now invests his powerful aspiration in order to reach some of the goals he neither knows nor understands, and his aspiration works like an "umbrella" which inspects all other desires to see if they serve the purpose. And if they don't, they are rejected with the comment that it would be a waste of time and energy to satisfy them.

This aspiration is really the ultimate desire, for the path of spiritual evolution will with unerring certainty lead to the complete elimination of the desire function as such, because it promotes separatism and selfishness, the most serious hindrances to spiritual development, which is about loving service to humanity and the world. And as it is the path of spiritual unfoldment the aspirant desires, what he is really feeling is the desire to end all desires.

Naturally, he is not aware of that in the beginning, but a time will come when he discovers that this is the way it has to be. It is a very painful recognition, because deep down he realizes that gratifying desire has given him the greatest pleasures in life. He now faces a situation similar to that of sitting on a branch of a tree and cutting it off between himself and the trunk. He knows that at some time or other he has cut through the branch, and then he is going to fall down! The personality falls down and perishes so that only the soul is left.

When the emotional life is focused in aspiration the state of consciousness develops through 3 stages:

1. Fiery longing for "liberation".
2. Intensive search for the inner reality behind outer phenomena.
3. Firm conviction of the existence of the soul, and obedience to its voice.

Alice A. Bailey says about the role of aspiration:

> *"It is well to point out here that this quality of 'going forth' towards the ideal or of straining towards the objective must be so profound in*

*the aspirant to yoga that no difficulties can turn him back. Only when this quality has been developed and proved and when it is found that no problem, no darkness and no time element can hinder, is a man permitted to become the disciple of some Master. Fiery effort, steady persistent longing and enduring faithfulness to the ideal visioned are the 'sine qua non'*[1] *of discipleship. These characteristics must be found in all three bodies, leading to the constant disciplining of the physical vehicle, the steady orientation of the emotional nature and the mental attitude which enables a man to 'count all things but loss'*[2] *if he can only arrive at his goal".*[3]

## Perseverance

The next quality meditation requires is perseverance – the rest of this life and probably also in many succeeding lives. Without this quality meditation will have no effect, and naturally this is bad news for those who begin on project meditation with the motto: "what's in it for me?" But this is just one of many examples of how the many techniques of the esoteric teaching are "self-protective". This means that in the long run they keep people away who do not yet have a motivation which can be brought to correspond with the deeper purposes of the teaching.

The esoteric teaching is characterized by always demanding a gigantic effort from the students without giving them the faintest idea of what they may expect in the other end – seen from an experiential point of view. They always work blindly in "anticipation of a grant", and the only thing which keeps them going in the beginning is aspiration. But if this is not strong enough, because the frustration which is experienced at the culmination of the personality is not sufficiently deep, nothing will come of the meditation effort. In most cases, this is probably entirely in accordance with the evolutionary perspective of the teaching, for it means that the people

[1] *Sine qua non*: "Without which not", indispensable condition.

[2] Philippians 3:8.

[3] Alice A. Bailey: *The Light of the Soul*, pp. 189-190.

concerned have not yet passed the phase of personality culmination, and therefore occult meditation may not represent the next step ahead for them.

We have to establish a steady meditation rhythm which is imprinted on the subconscious and becomes a habit, for the habit saves us a lot of conscious disciplining. The effect of the habit is that if we don't meditate we feel that something is missing, and in this way meditation becomes more than just a spiritual discipline – it becomes a daily sacrament[1] where we tune into the rhythm of the world, as Michal Eastcott says.

Therefore, we should be patient and not think that we are busy, for busyness disturbs the process. It shows that our motive is desire for results and not affinity to the soul and the service work it tries to manifest. We should understand the occult saying, "make haste slowly", for a thorough development of each stage speeds up the process in the long run. It is like painting an apartment. We finish up faster if we make a solid first coating. I think every painter will agree to that.

## Concentration

Another quality which is required is concentration, that is, the ability to collect the thoughts in a focal point. Thereby, the effectiveness of the thought process is increased, in the same way as we may increase the effect of the sunbeams by focusing them through a burning-glass. The importance of concentration in meditation is emphasized by Alice A. Bailey:

> *"Meditation is but the extension of concentration and grows out of the facility a man achieves in 'fixing the mind' at will on any particular object. It falls under the same rules and conditions as concentration and the only distinction between the two is in the time element. Having achieved the capacity to focus the mind steadily upon an ob-*

[1] *Sacrament*: Ceremony regarded as an outward sign of an inward and spiritual grace.

*ject, the next step is developing the power to hold the mind stuff or chitta unwaveringly occupied with that object or thought for a prolonged period".*[1]

During concentration, all other activities of the mind are automatically kept quiet. So, we do not use specific methods like mantras to still the mind, that is, strings of words which, in order to put all other thoughts to flight, are repeated automatically. These methods may be dangerous, for they lead the mind into a passive susceptibility amounting almost to trance. We will deal with this susceptibility later under the heading of "Elements of Danger".

But we may illustrate the use of mantras with an image. Imagine a man sitting in an empty room with a number of doors. Each time a door opens he rushes up to close it. Otherwise, he doesn't do anything, and therefore nothing comes of the process.

So, meditation is a clear and concise thought process which at some time leads to clear results and not vague and nebulous conceptions, as some may believe. This is demonstrated by those individuals who have reached the goal, obtained brain conscious soul contact and now make the results of their meditations available for other people. They don't meditate any longer but communicate through contemplation[2] with the higher self, and through it with the Ashram. This phenomenon Alice A. Bailey has commented on in the following manner:

*"An initiate never meditates. The advanced disciple never meditates; he does not need to. He has an instinctual contact, and the instinctual memory works. If you are using recollection, you are drawing the mind back into the personality life, and the initiate is not interested in the personality life in any way. He does not need to be… Meditation is entirely confined to mental processes, and he only uses the mind to convey thoughtforms. The initiate contemplates, which means that he assumes a point of direction; he is directing all the time the ener-*

[1] Alice A. Bailey: *The Light of the Soul*, p. 247.

[2] This state will be thoroughly dealt with in a later chapter.

*gies that bring about what happens in the three worlds. In order to meditate you have to work with the mental apparatus in the three worlds".*[1]

The word "ashram" is Sanskrit and means a "sacred building", but in modern esoteric teaching it is used to denote the field of consciousness which arises when a Master synchronizes the consciousness of all his co-workers with his own.

There are 2 kinds of concentration:

*Spontaneous and automatic concentration,* which is the natural outcome when that which we are dealing with interests us. The thought is really obeying an emotional motivation, namely, the desire for that which interests us, and that causes the suspense which casts a spell over us.

*Conscious and directed concentration.* This is something consciousness is instructed to do by the self or "I". It is experienced as boring and unattractive by the emotions who by nature try to distract it by using the imagination to produce images far more appealing.

But when the self is able to concentrate consciously for longer periods of time the process proceeds through 7 phases:

1. Choice of object to concentrate on.
2. Withdrawal of the mind from the periphery of the vehicle, so that all outer impressions are precluded and consciousness is no longer outgoing.
3. Centering of consciousness in the head.
4. Application of the mind on the chosen object.
5. Visualization of the object.
6. Extension of the mental concepts which have been formed from the specific and particular to more general and universal concepts.
7. Attempt to reach that which lies behind the form, that is, the idea which is responsible for the form.[2]

[1] Alice A. Bailey: Article, March 12, 1943. Published on the website of the School for Esoteric Studies.

[2] Alice A. Bailey: *The Light of the Soul*, p. 244, edited & adapted.

## The Mind – an Independent Being

Many people are not able to concentrate for a longer period of time. They have to practise. That it is difficult to concentrate is due to the fact that the mind – that is, the consciousness in the mental body – in some regards acts as an independent being who has other intentions than we who use it.

The reason is that the mental body contains a type of substance esoterically termed "elemental essence". If we want to understand what that is we have to glance at evolution as it is here on planet earth.

Seen in the big perspective, we may say that evolution proceeds in the following manner: pure life energy streams forth or "down" from its cosmic source to meet "substance" or "matter" in order to evolve consciousness, which can be said to be the ability to vibrate matter. This begins in the mineral kingdom on the physical plane where there are dense forms in which life can incarnate for a long time. But on the way "down" from its spiritual "heights", the life energy forms big clouds of a fleeting substance on the inner planes, holding them together by its magnetism. These clouds are termed "elemental essence".

The life energy cannot develop consciousness in the elemental essence because it has not yet learned how to make the essence oscillate. This is what it is about to learn by gathering the clouds about itself and through them register the vibrations of the individual particles of substance.

Therefore, elemental essence has a natural tendency to make for accumulations of substance – that is, bodies – which are inhabited by living beings who are able to create strong vibrations by their states of consciousness, and here, clearly, the mental bodies of human beings are the best places to be.

As man employs his mental body by building its substance into thoughtforms depicting what he is thinking of, he cannot avoid drawing some of the essence from the mental body as a whole into the thoughtforms. This is the optimal position for the elemental essence, for a thoughtform receives the most intense oscillations a person is capable of. The problem is that thoughtforms gradually die out as the level of energy decreases, and the only way by which the essence can prevent the thoughtforms from disintegrating is to make the person repeat the thought behind the form. If the essence succeeds, the form receives an injection of energy and may continue to exist for a while.

This means that in the mental body of a human being there are numerous thoughtforms containing elemental essence, and that the essence in each form is queuing up to have its thought repeated and thereby live longer in its privileged position. This makes the mind restless, for each time we are done with a thought immediately another thought wants to be registered on the "scoreboard" – not because we as human beings need or want the thought, but because the elemental essence wants to stay in its vibrating environment.

That is why we may say that the mind has its own "identity" and inclinations quite independently of the soul who also inhabits the body.

Therefore, it is not wise to begin a meditation by trying to establish quiet and stillness, for it is the worst conceivable condition for the elemental essence and will surely awaken its resistance. Instead, we should use our esoteric knowledge and cooperate with the mind by beginning the meditation with intensive thought activity. Thus we utilize the qualities of the mental body, and at the same time we direct and control it. Then later we may "slip in" the stillness which is necessary if we want to realize the higher purpose of the meditation.

But let us try out a brief exercise which demonstrates our ability to concentrate:

### Exercise in Concentration

Straighten your back, close your eyes, and relax the body completely... Call forth the image of a *screw* in your mind. Enlarge it in proportion to yourself... Float about it and follow the spiral of the screw thread in close-up... See the notch and "fly" down through it like a fighter plane in a Star Wars movie... Determine in advance a definite period of time you want to spend on this exercise. Finish it, and return to the normal waking consciousness.

## Visualization

The next quality we need to have if we want to meditate is the ability to visualize. All the meditation processes must and will embody visualization as a primary step for the following reasons:

1. Visualization demonstrates the occult law that "energy follows and adjust itself to thought". *Visualization of images* focuses thought within the head at a point midway between the pituitary body and the pineal gland. Here we create pictures of things we desire and intend to work for. *Visualization of the direction of energy* focuses thought in the area directly around the pineal gland. This turns the pineal gland into the centre of a magnetic field which is set in motion by the power of visualization. It enables the aspirant to gather energy and direct it with intention to one or other of the centers, inevitably producing results within the etheric body.[1]

[1] *Etheric body*: Energy field which penetrates the physical cell body and stretches a couple of centimetres outside.

2. Visualization is the form-building aspect of the creative imagination. The process falls into 3 parts: (1) the *gathering* of energy-substance with a frequency which is suited for the form that is going to be built, (2) the *focusing* of the energy according to the intention, and (3) the *dispatch* of the energy by means of the pictorial process in any desired direction – that is, to certain centers in a certain order.
3. Visualization helps us to distinguish between truth and falsity. The creative imagination visualizes a form and the thought energy gives the form life and direction. Thereby, a bridge is built between the astral and mental bodies, and this becomes a triple line of energy when the soul utilizes the creative process in a planned and constructive manner so that the form embodies a definite purpose.[1]

During meditation, visualization serves 2 purposes: (1) to build and maintain the conceptions of the meditation, and (2) to receive and convert the impulses received during meditation into thought-forms, so that they are available for the service work.

But here we should be aware of the fact that the imagination is primarily linked to the desire aspect of the emotions. It is simply the tool which desire employs to build images of the things it must come to a decision on. For instance, if we want something nice to eat we send the imagination off to the refrigerator or pantry to see if there is something we would fancy to eat. The imagination returns to the desire and presents it with pictures it can weigh up. The result is a reward in the form of something delicious we would like to eat or drink at that particular time.

This means that if we want to use visualization – and with it, imagination – in meditation we have to liberate the imagination from desire by renouncing the reward. Naturally, emotion will resist, for this means that the imagination has to work free of charge and that is not in the interest of desire. Seen from the point of view of desire, the goal and meaning of life is the reward, so why renounce it? But the problem is that as emotion has a firm grip on the imagination

[1] See Alice A. Bailey: *Discipleship in the New Age I*, pp. 89-91.

it will use it to produce pictures which are serious competitors to those the meditation requires. That is why it is so difficult to visualize the mental images which are prescribed in meditation forms.

So, we must be on our guard not to be carried away by the imagination. Consciously and with an act of will we get it started at building the forms we need, but all the time we keep the process under observation and control it with the will. We simply give it a little leash, as when we walk the dog and give it a little leash every time it wants to sniff at things, but never so much that it loses its way deeply into the bushes.

But let us see what it is like to visualize. I have chosen an environment everybody knows, so if you can't remember the exact wording you can always piece something together yourself.

### Exercise in Visualization

Straighten your back, close your eyes, and relax the body... Imagine that you go for a walk in the forest a spring day. You have chosen a forest where the ground is a bit broken so that the visual angle changes every time the path turns... Suddenly you see an inviting clearing with a log you can sit on. You sit down and start to notice all the details in the surroundings: the forest floor with its withered leaves from last season, flowers and little bushes making their way into the life-giving atmosphere, snails and thousands of insects fighting for the best prey, and birds singing their mysterious songs... Feel the warmth from the sun shining through the foliage, listen to the monotonous and indefinable sound from the many living creatures, each having its own little will, and enjoy the fragrance of growth and evaporation...

Decide a definite amount of time you want to spend on the exercise, and then take the image out of your head.

# Meditation

Now is the time for the meditation process itself. We will begin with a few basic reflections which clarify the entire subject. Meditation is the primary foundation for that which is called "spiritual development". If we want to understand that statement we have to go back in evolution and take a rapid glance at the birth of human consciousness at the transition from the animal to the human kingdom.

In the beginning, consciousness was entirely focused on physical existence. All emotional and mental states were responses to sense impressions and dealt with the basic necessities of life: food, warmth, and sex. Not until man had learnt to do well in nature and didn't have to use his entire capacity to survive was it possible to develop a real thought life or intellect which could function independently of sense impressions, instincts, and emotions.

At first, man uses his intellect to study his surroundings and draw conclusions as to the various regularities he observes in nature. But in connection to this process he starts to get ideas which originate in the world of the soul. This means that the soul responds to the deliberations of the intellect and helps by inspiring it. These thought processes we may very well call "meditation", for also later in the process it is the purpose of meditation to establish contact from the physical waking consciousness to the soul, and later to the spirit or higher self.

Here we should notice that what we call "consciousness" – that is, the ability to perceive and apprehend – is always a response from "inner instances" to what is going on in "outer instances", and once the human personality, with its integration of thoughts, emotions, and actions is established, it is the personality as a whole that constitutes the "outer instance", while the "inner instance" is the soul in its own world. Thereby, what we call consciousness becomes a direct expression of the soul, and meditation is its most natural activity – the lifeblood of the consciousness aspect.

Therefore, we can say that meditation is a technical process whereby the human personality contacts the soul and invokes an inflow of its energies, so that the soul-infused personality emerges. Thus, the qualities of the soul are embodied in the 3 worlds of the personality and can be utilized in the service work in 2 ways:

- Through the soul we can focus on the plan of evolution as it exists in the consciousness of the Hierarchy and help realizing it in society.

- Through the soul we may intuit spiritual ideas and concepts and transfer them to the collective mind of humanity where they become available to thinking people as their own. In this way, these people are also enabled to serve the plan of evolution – even if it is unconsciously.

The process of meditation itself proceeds through several well-defined phases which are best illustrated on a drawing – see Figure 5.

## Alignment

The phases are depicted on an arc to show that there is an ascent and a descent in the process. Therefore, we find the first phase down to the left on the drawing, and it consists in a coordination of the elements of consciousness. When we begin the meditation we are focused in the physical waking consciousness, and this should now be coordinated with the inner psychic states of consciousness, that is, the frequency pattern of the physical body has to be attuned to the frequency patterns of the inner bodies of emotion and thought. Here are 2 stages:

1. *Alignment of the 3 personality vehicles mutually* so that we don't think one thing, feel another, and do a third. As to energy, the personality should be a coherent factor, for otherwise it cannot polarize its energy ("electrically") to that of the soul, so that a field of tension is established in which the work can be done. If a carriage is to move forward, the 3 horses drawing it must move in the same direction.
2. *Alignment of the integrated personality with the soul.* Since the energy of the soul has a far higher frequency level than that of the brain, the latter must be emptied of its ordinary, temporal content and elevated to its highest level.

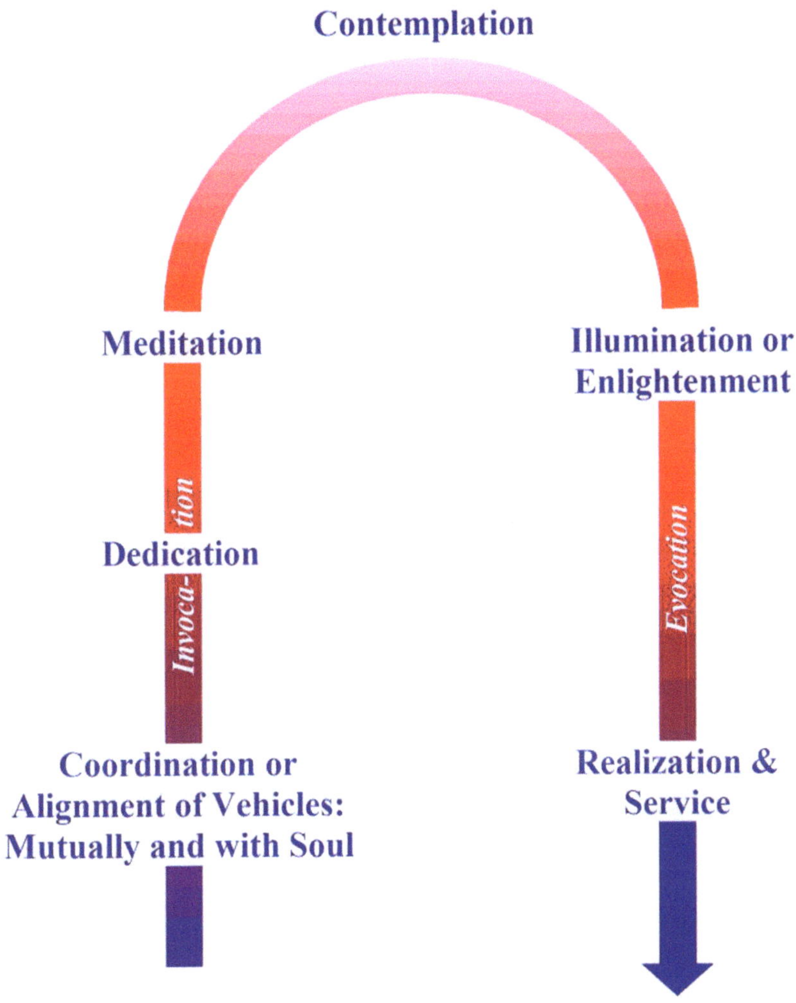


Figure 5

The best illustration we may give of this alignment process is a meditation, for nothing can replace the experiential dimension we enter when we perform exercises of that kind.

## Meditation – Alignment

***Physical body***

Sit comfortably, straighten the back, and close your eyes... Turn your attention to the body and go over in your mind all the groups of muscles, from the feet to the head. Make sure that all muscles relax – even the neck, the eyes, and the tongue. The body should be balanced and resting, but at the same time sensitive, conscious, and alert.

***Etheric body and breath***

Concentrate on your breath now. Count 1-2-3 when you inhale and 4-5-6 when you exhale... Make the rhythm a little slower, while the breath is still easy and effortless... When the rhythm is steady and stable, stop counting. Make sure that it doesn't become a habit which is going on in the background of consciousness while you try to concentrate on the next step.

***Emotional body***

Turn the attention to the emotional nature... Let the emotions become quiescent and try not to "must" or "will" anything... Feel the sense of well-being and that you may safely withdraw from this dimension of your being. It will not call attention to itself or try to hold you in the world of sensation.

***Mental body***

Now lead your attention into the world of thought... See how remembrances and associations come and go on the periphery while you penetrate to the core of the mind – the eye of the storm. Here clarity and transparency prevail and you experience an intensity which is not related to activity but to being.

***Integration***
Finally, imagine that a pure white light flows from the soul into your consciousness – cleansing, stabilizing, and calming it. Rest in this state of mind and say with conviction:

> *More radiant than the sun, purer than the snow, subtler than the ether is the Self, The spirit within me. I am that Self. That Self am I.*[1]

## Dedication

After coordination follows "dedication". We simply dedicate the meditation to a definite purpose. Some meditation teachers find this to be "old-fashioned", but I think we should be aware of the fact that it may be an important driving force to clarify the intention and goal.

Focusing on the intention not only gathers the forces of the personality together, but it also invokes the will. We may say that the dedication is a sort of an arrow we let off so that it draws the rest of the content with it. In the heart of the dedication we find the aspiration which is our striving for spiritual development. Without this, there is nothing – as we have seen previously.

The dedication may take different forms and be directed toward various goals, such as the soul, the ashram, or humanity as a whole. We find a very beautiful illustration in the meditation many aspirants all around the world use every Thursday.[2] It is a meditation where we are offered the opportunity to help in the preparations for the reappearance of the Christ, and maybe that is why the dedication has such a unique atmosphere:

[1] Alice A. Bailey: *From Intellect to Intuition*, p. 228.

[2] Because Thursday is a 2nd-ray day, the ray of the department of the Christ. A "ray" is a primary energy in our world, influencing all life and all evolution. There are 7 rays in all.

*"Forgetting the things which lie behind, I will strive towards my higher spiritual possibilities. I dedicate myself anew to the service of the Coming One and will do all I can to prepare men's minds and hearts for that event. I have no other life intention".*[1]

## Meditation

Now we come to the phase in the meditation process which is actually called "meditation". Here we distinguish between 2 primary types, but there are no clear lines of demarcation, for at a certain point the 2 meditations merge into one another. Still, it is wise to keep them separated in the beginning so that we preserve our overview:

*Meditation with seed thought.* This is a process where we think about a definite theme, sentence, or word. It is the simplest form of meditation and very well suited as a beginning, because it employs the ordinary, active, and directed thinking which the mind or mental body is accustomed to. The Tibetan says about it that it concerns "the formation of thoughts," and "the bringing down to the concrete levels of the mental plane, of abstract ideas and intuitions."

*Meditation without seed thought.* This is a process where the mind is kept quiet and attentive so that it is able to receive inspiration which sheds fresh light on a definite theme – or any theme – that is decided by the source of inspiration. It may be compared to the picking up of a sound from afar. The Tibetan says about it that it concerns the "aligning of the ego," and "the creation of that vacuum betwixt the physical brain and the Ego,[2] which results in the divine outpouring, and the consequent shattering of the forms and subsequent liberation."[3]

[1] Alice A. Bailey: *Discipleship in the New Age II*, pp. 226-227.

[2] In this context, the word "Ego" is synonymous with the Soul, the true Self.

[3] Alice A. Bailey: *Letters on Occult Meditation*, p. 58.

## Meditation with Seed Thought

As we have seen, the theme we want to focus on during meditation is chosen in advance and termed a "seed thought" because it is a seed which can shoot and bloom during the process. We think about all aspects of it, and at the same time we see to it that we do not move too far away from the theme.

Naturally, there must be room for associations and intuitive ideas, but it may be difficult to determine whether a thought which does not seem to have an obvious relation to the seed thought is an expression of inspiration, or if it is merely a demonstration of the imagination following an impulse because it is not really interested in the meditation. That is why we have to keep a certain order by constantly getting back to the theme and relating the ideas to it, and at the same time be careful not to stifle the inspiration and intuition.

The reflections on the seed thought should not take more than 5-10 minutes, but then the seed thought is repeated many times over – for instance every morning for a month.

As to the results, we should be aware of the fact that the mind, as mentioned above, usually serves the emotional nature. In most situations, we use thought to figure out how we may satisfy our desires. If we want to travel – that is, a desire – we ask the mind to get the money, and within a couple of years we may have saved the necessary amount because the mind made a plan which lead to that result.

The same applies to the work we live by. We don't go to work every day because we have a burning desire to build, sell, administrate, or whatever it is we do for a living, but because we want to make money for our subsistence and pleasures.

Therefore, it may be difficult to get the mind to work in its own dimension and directed by the will. It cannot be done by just one attempt, and this means that it may take some time before the meditation renders noticeable results.

Neither should we expect that the ideas, which eventually do show up, have anything to do with the seed thought. It is not the purpose of a meditation with seed thought to be an "extended" form of research where we use meditative states of consciousness to get deeper into our subject.

Naturally, it often happens that the meditation enriches the perception of the seed thought and clarifies the questions which almost always turn up. But it may as well be that the seed thought just acted as a catalyst for entirely different ideas which have exerted a certain pressure from the dimension of the soul, but which we have been blocking with our commonsensical intellect. So, here we should not be too rigorous in our supervision of the thought processes. That is why the whole process is really entrusted to the intuition, for it is the deeper purpose of meditation to develop the higher spiritual intuition, and that is obvious from a fairly early stage.

In many cases, we do not think that the fragmentary results we get from our meditation work are significant in themselves. But after some time, we discover that although we may not have had many new ideas, new combinations of existing thoughts and concepts have arisen. In this way, our entire spectrum is expanded and this is just as important for our perception as new ideas.

Most people are familiar with that which is called an "aha experience". It is a sudden and profound understanding which appears in our consciousness, and it gives us great joy and a sense of integration and wholeness. We have understood! But when we take a closer look at what it really is we have understood, it often turns out to be things we already knew and that what is new is merely a small turn of an element which makes the entirety appear as new.

This is a very important process for some of the greatest and most significant truths are really staring us in our face, and all that we need is a small turn of our own attitude which is the only thing standing in the way of a profound realization that may change life, not only for ourselves but also for others who have had the same problem.

Another reaction many people have to a meditation with a seed thought is that they think the theme is exhausted after a very short time of deliberations. This is usually due to the fact that they are not going far enough into the seed thought, and that fundamentally they may not be very interested in meditation at that moment.

For instance, the seed thought may say, "I seek to love, not hate." At first sight this seems to be a very simple seed thought and we may not think that there is much to ponder on. Normally, we are quite nice guys who only want the best for other people, so, what's the problem? But if we think it over there are many questions we could ask ourselves. What is love really? Is it a cause and consequently an emotion, or is it the effect of a deep intuitive insight which only expresses itself as love when it enters the emotional body? What kind of people are easy for us to love, and what aren't? What prevents me from always loving everybody? And similarly with hate. What disguises does hate hide behind? Is it all kinds of hate I am free of? Do I not even hate those who hurt me? Wouldn't it actually be fair?, etc.

Naturally, we are not able to think of all the details in a single meditation, and that is one of the reasons why it is important to repeat seed thoughts and work with them for a longer period of time.

Other examples of seed thoughts may be: "Be joyful, for joy lets in the light", "harmlessness is not negativity, but perfect poise" or "the will-to-good is the magnetic seed of the future".[1] In all these cases, we are immediately able to understand the meaning of the sentence itself, so that the primary difficulty lies in the "depth" of the individual parts, as we saw in the previous example of "I seek to love, not hate."

But there is another kind of seed thought where it is difficult to find any immediate meaning in the sentence. This is the so-called paradoxes[2] containing apparent contradictions which can only be united if a synthesis is found on a higher and more comprehensive plane. We find the most extreme examples in Zen Buddhist literature, as for instance: "to suffer joyfully" – which does not mean to rejoice at suffering as the masochist does – "make haste slowly", "live in the eternal and in the moment", or "see activity in inactivity and inactivity in activity."

But anyway, a seed thought is always a "form", whether it is a "word form" or and "image form", and therefore it is in the nature of a symbol which may be interpreted in 3 ways:[3]

[1] Michal Eastcott: *The Silent Path*, p. 96.

[2] Greek: Contrary to accepted opinion.

[3] Alice A. Bailey: *From Intellect to Intuition*, pp. 113-115, edited & adapted.

*Objective interpretation,* which describes the "outer" form and function of the symbol. The form serves 2 purposes: (1) to give a hint as to the idea behind the form. This connects the symbol with the mental plane but does not liberate it from the 3 worlds of the personality. (2) To limit the idea so that it suits the level of human evolution.

*Subjective interpretation,* which sees the meaning of, or the idea behind, the symbol. This enables us to interpret the happenings in the world. For instance, the American declaration of independence was seen as a heroic deed by the Americans and a treachery by the English. In the world of meaning, humanity takes a major step towards an understanding of the concept of "freedom." Therefore, the world of meaning is the dimension of ideas or the soul.

*Spiritual interpretation,* which finds the purpose behind the idea, the central dynamic energy that is responsible for the subjective activity and its objective form. It expresses the spiritual purpose of things in the plan of evolution and is therefore related to the dimension of the higher self.

From the long-term point of view, it is the intention that all these 3 ways of interpretation should be used on the seed thought, but this is today impossible for most people. All that we can do is to use the first two methods and then postpone the third for a future incarnation, for it requires that the disciple has reached the very advanced level esoterically termed the 3rd initiation.[1]

But let us see how a meditation with seed thought works. I have chosen an old theme which has probably been used in many schools of meditation. It is called "The Master in the Heart" and is based on the fact that there is a direct connection between the 12-petalled lotus of the soul on the higher mental plane and our physical-etheric heart chakra, which is also a 12-petalled lotus, situated on the front of the etheric body off the heart. A 12-petalled lotus is always a channel for the energy we normally call "love". This means that the energy our soul primarily transmits is spiritual love-wisdom, as it streams forth from the buddhic world, and that it is the task of the heart centre to lead this energy from the soul into our physical

[1] *Initiation*: Name for a well defined spiritual level of evolution.

consciousness. But at the same time, the soul is also the access to the Master in the Hierarchy, and in this way the meditation gets a double meaning.

### Meditation with Seed Thought

*Preparation*
Sit comfortably, and relax the body. Feel that the chair carries your weight. Straighten the back, and close your eyes. Rest arms and legs in a natural way. Take a deep breath, and then forget all about the breath.

*Integration*
Imagine that the 3 bodies of your personality – the physical, emotional, and mental body – are aligned with each other and function as a unity. Furthermore, imagine that this integrated unity is sensitive to the energies entering from the soul.

*Affirmation*
Now affirm that you are a soul-infused personality by saying the mantra of the disciple:

*I am a point of light within a greater Light.*
*I am a strand of loving energy within the stream of Love divine.*
*I am a point of sacrificial Fire, focused within the fiery Will of God.*
*And thus I stand.*

*I am a way by which men may achieve.*
*I am a source of strength, enabling them to stand.*
*I am a beam of light, shining upon their way.*
*And thus I stand.*

*And standing thus, I revolve*
*And tread this way, the ways of men,*
*And know the ways of God.*
*And thus I stand.*

***Visualization***

Picture the etheric heart centre as a small blue sphere in the region between the shoulder blades. See how it is connected with a folded golden lotus on the front of the etheric body off the heart. Imagine that the light of the soul flows down through the top of the head and into the golden lotus where it makes it unfold. Build now with loving dedication a picture of the Master in the heart and visualize that he represents all that you perceive as noble and spiritual.

***Meditation with seed thought***

Raise your consciousness into the head and meditate on the seed thought for 5-10 minutes. It goes:

> *The soul is one in all my fellow human beings and I am one with them.*

***Conclusion***

Return to your ordinary physical consciousness. If you feel like it you may write down your impressions from the meditation, so that later on you can compare them with other impressions.

## Meditation without Seed Thought

We may obtain a clear understanding of the difference between this meditation and the previous one by regarding the mind as an "inner eye". In a meditation with a seed thought, this eye looks "horizontally" out on the surroundings, that is, the theme or seed thought, while in a meditation without a seed thought, it looks vertically upwards and tries to distinguish that which belongs to a dimension that is higher than the mind's own plane.

This type of meditation is far more difficult and may only be practiced by people with a good deal of experience in the field, because the mind is kept quiet in a state of "tension" while the meditator awaits response from the soul and the spirit, and that is difficult to do without straining the brain and nervous system.

The meditation consists in the generation of an extreme sensitivity and responsiveness which is directed inwardly toward the soul and the higher self. At the same time, all impulses from "without" are screened off – that is, the thoughts and emotions from our own inner bodies and those of other people which constantly surround us – while we keep the personality at such a high vibrational level that it is able to respond to the high frequency energies of the soul.

Here we should notice that impulses from the higher part of the mental plane, which is the home of abstract thought, and the dimension above, the buddhic world with its pure intuitive reason, are formless or "arupa" as it is called with an old theosophical Sanskrit designation. They are in the nature of radiation and not images.

This means that if the impressions we receive during meditation are filled with colors, pictures, and/or people they don't originate in the world of the soul but in the astral world. That is why during the process we have to have a subtle distinction between passive receptivity and mental creativity.

The receptivity is necessary if we want to receive the spiritual impulses, and the creativity is necessary for the formulation of the impulses by the analytical mind so that they may be available for the service work. But if the receptiveness is too extensive we run the risk of withdrawing altogether from the physical brain consciousness. It is said that Abraham Maslow, one of the most gifted psychiatrists of our time, was liable to have amnesia every time he "returned" to the body from his profound creative reflections. If true, this may be an example of the above mechanism. If the creativity is too predominant we run the risk of over-interpreting the impressions from the meditation so that it is really our own imagination which produces the result.

So, during the process there is a sort of "condensed" emptiness, or thought-free consciousness as Michal Eastcott calls it, pregnant with "potential" energy which can seize and interpret impulses normally beyond the range of our consciousness.

However, the use of the word "emptiness" has made some people believe that it is a passive emptiness which can be produced by means of mantras. But this kind of emptiness may be dangerous because it is an open invitation to obsession.[1] Apart from this, there is a certain probability that the impressions received during meditation will be purely astral and instrumental in wrapping the meditator in a cloud of glamour so dense that it threatens to destroy the entire meditation work. For the glamour will often be of such a nature that it makes the aspirant see himself as chosen for a spiritual destiny with all the arrogance that entails. Then he has 2 problems: he must get rid of the glamour before he can move on, and he must start the meditation work all over.

This is a big problem today because many people use meditation systems which may have those very effects, and since the visions the meditators obtain tend to be euphoric, alluring, and stimulating for their self-esteem it is almost impossible for such meditators to wrench themselves free and start on a constructive form of meditation which calls forth the aspiration and humility necessary for developing contact with the soul, and through it the Ashram and the Hierarchy.

When we use a meditation without a seed thought it often happens that we are not conscious of the impression we receive right away. There is a huge frequency leap between the soul and the personality, and therefore it may be very difficult for the brain to

[1] *Obsession*: The invasion of a physical body by a discarnated being.

perceive the formless soul impulses in such a clear way that they take shape. Often, we need a definite association to release the impression and maybe it does not show until a day or two. Then we may have one of those "aha experiences", mentioned above, in the middle of a pedestrian crossing, so that all the cars hoot and honk because we stopped in the middle of the "rapture".

It must have been this mechanism which made Beethoven say that it is crime against humanity for a creative person to take a walk without bringing a pad and a pencil. Imagine if we had missed the 9th symphony for that reason!

This is also why we sometimes don't get the answer to a question we ask at night, just before falling asleep, until a couple of days later. The dimension we visit during the sleep of the body presents ample opportunities to find the answer to almost any question, and the process is really fairly simple. During sleep, we go to see the person or persons who can help us with the answer, whether it is one of the astral or mental "universities" where teaching is offered during night time, an expert in the field, or, for disciples, the Ashram. But the big difference in frequency between the inner dimensions of consciousness and the physical brain awareness, and the fact that the inner worlds have more than the 3 dimensions of space we know from the physical world, will often give us problems in the transference so that there is a delay in the reception.

When we use this meditation, and after the introductory stages, we enter into the reception phase itself. Here the first requirement is absolute stillness, for the reception of spiritual impulses and the transference of them to the personal consciousness presupposes that all thoughtforms which may stand in the way are "deactivated". Naturally, this involves a constant effort, for the mind is not used to that condition and will all along try to escape by offering entertainment in the form of appealing thoughtforms. In his book *The Act of Will*, the Italian psychiatrist Roberto Assagioli gives a cheerful illustration of this:

*"I was immersed in a profound meditation and knew that I had reached a limpid, radiant state, when this thought crossed my mind: 'I know I am at this level, and yet I am deaf and blind and can hear*

*and see nothing.' A moment passed and then this humorous reply came: 'If you were silent as well, you would be able to see and hear'".*[1]

In the receptive state, there are various ways in which we may experience the soul or higher self. As the mind to a certain extent may be regarded as an inner "eye" a visual impression is the most common, but we should always remember that it is abstractions and not images which are received, and therefore a visual impression really means understanding or insight. We "see" the solution to a problem or get a "brilliant" idea.

The experience may also come through the sense of hearing, but again it is not ordinary sound impressions, like voices or music, but abstract units of meaning of a symbolic character. Here, too, Assagioli gives us a good example in the form of the message Saint Francis of Assisi received, "go, Francis, and repair my house". Ostensibly, this is about rebuilding an old and tumbledown church on the physical plane, but deep down it concerns the entire foundation of faith in the Christian church.

A third form of impression is related to the sense of touch. This is not some concrete meaning which is transferred, but the aspirant senses some kind of "spiritual presence" which enables him to identify with a spiritual reality and be receptive to its qualities. The experience harmonizes, vitalizes, and stimulates him with energy.

After the receptive phase follows the registering of the impression. The analytical mind builds a thoughtform which fits in with the rest of the mind's content. Here it is wise to write the impression down as soon as possible, for nothing fades so quickly in the ordinary waking consciousness as intuitive impressions.

But it may also be that nothing happens, and that is disappointing to many people. There are various reasons for that. The impression may be delayed, as mentioned above, but the most important here, I think, is the fact that it takes many incarnations to become a virtuoso in meditation, for developing brain conscious contact with the higher self, which is the final goal, is really a feat of strength which involves far more than just doing the morning meditation every day.

[1] Roberto Assagioli: *The Act of Will*, p. 224.

It requires discipline in order to refine the substance of the bodies and thereby raise their vibratory level. At the same time, we have to become conscious of our entire energy balance so that we don't waste energy on non-essentials whether it is physical activities or unnecessary states of consciousness. I think most people are aware of the amount of energy spent on a single fit of rage, or the exudation involved when we bear a grudge against somebody, are jealous or envious. All this has to be brought to an end through character development plus the 3 disciplines which characterize discipleship living: meditation, study, and service.

It should be clear that if we are in an incarnation where this long evolutionary development is about to begin it is very limited what we may expect from our meditation work. But in the last analysis, this is not important, for we have to begin at some time, and if it is not in this life time it will be in a later incarnation. So, why not take the opportunity now that it presents itself to us? We cannot change our spiritual level or status here and now – that is what the whole process is about – but we can always take the first step, and even if there are no obvious results from the meditation work there will be a gradual strengthening of the character, a gradual refinement of the bodies, and a gradual polarization of the consciousness in ever higher regions.

Very often, the effect of meditation is something which other people notice more clearly than ourselves, for our self-awareness is a continuous process where it is difficult to recognize little changes, whereas others only see us from time to time and therefore are witnessing greater leaps.

But let us see how a receptive meditation without a seed thought works out in practice. In the beginning, there is not much difference between this and the one with a seed thought, because the introductory phases are necessary in any case. We always have to find a comfortable position to sit in, and we need to integrate the personality and connect it with the dimension of the soul – as far as we can. Therefore, I have deliberately chosen to make the first part of the meditation identical with the one with a seed thought so that it is easier to see the difference by comparing the last part of both meditations.

## Meditation without Seed Thought

*Preparation*
Sit comfortably, and relax the body. Feel that the chair carries your weight. Straighten the back, and close your eyes. Rest arms and legs in a natural way. Take a deep breath, and then forget all about the breath.

*Integration*
Imagine that the 3 bodies of your personality – the physical, emotional and mental body – are aligned with each other and function as a unity. Furthermore, imagine that this integrated unity is sensitive to the energies entering from the soul.

*Affirmation*
Now affirm that you are a soul-infused personality by saying the mantra of the disciple:

*I am a point of light within a greater Light.*
*I am a strand of loving energy within the stream of Love divine.*
*I am a point of sacrificial Fire, focused within the fiery Will of God.*
*And thus I stand.*

*I am a way by which men may achieve.*
*I am a source of strength, enabling them to stand.*
*I am a beam of light, shining upon their way.*
*And thus I stand.*

*And standing thus, I revolve*
*And tread this way, the ways of men,*
*And know the ways of God.*
*And thus I stand.*

Imagine that a pure white light is pouring down from the dimensions of the soul and the spirit into the threefold personality, cleansing, stabilizing and illuminating the entire field of consciousness. Then say in you mind with emphasis and meaning:

> *May the energy of the divine Self inspire me and the light of the soul direct. Lead me, O Lord, from darkness to Light, from the unreal to the Real, from death to Immortality.*

***Visualization***

Visualize a quiet and peaceful forest lake an early summers morning. See the surrounding trees casting their shadows on the surface so that only a limited space is free to mirror the light of the sky. Be aware that the capability of the lake to reflect the surroundings is a perfect image of the type of receptiveness you want to establish in relation to the impulses from the soul and higher self, and realize that it is only able to do so when the surface is absolutely still and limpid. Now imagine that you lean forward so that you see your own face reflected by the water. Continue the movement until your lips touch the surface so that in one radiant moment of blissful beatitude your lower and higher selves merge into one another and become one.

***Reception***

Be absolutely still, while you control the mind and hold your consciousness open to impressions that might leave a mark on the mind substance (chitta). Be at the same time aware of the subject you want to have elucidated. Be positive, alert and mentally silent while you listen to the faint sound from far away.

***Anchoring***
Now bring down into the analytical mind the impressions you have had. Be careful that you are meticulous in the way you give them form so that it is not your imagination which produces the result. Meditate reflectively on them for a time so that they are really anchored in your consciousness and you are able to remember every detail afterwards.

***Conclusion***
Return to your ordinary physical consciousness and write the impressions down so that they contribute to your storehouse of experienced knowledge.

## Creative Meditation

Roberto Assagioli, who is known for his work with psychosynthesis, and who, incidentally, was a disciple of the Tibetan Master, introduced 3 types of meditation. That is, one more than we have been dealing with previously:

1. Reflective meditation which is meditation with seed thought.
2. Receptive meditation which is meditation without seed thought.
3. Creative meditation.

Creative meditation may be used in several ways, but the most common is refinement of the personality. We want to increase the weight of our positive qualities in relation to the negative ones, and we do that by building thoughtforms which can contribute to the strength and influence of the spiritual dimensions. It is not always necessary to build these forms from the bottom. They already exist, and then the task consists in stimulating their influence. If, for instance, the qualities of peace, devotion, or compassion are considered, we can be sure that they have existed in higher spheres for a long time.

The meditation itself is a combination of the two original types of meditation, where the first half is reflective and deals with the gathering of concepts and ideas into one thoughtform, while the other half consists in holding this thoughtform in the light from higher dimensions in order to draw high-frequency energy "down" into the form and perhaps also new ideas which may extend the perspective.

This form of meditation is used by many aspirants in relation to the 6 laws and principles which are going to characterize the future civilization and culture. As a matter of fact, the Tibetan requested that groups were formed which could carry out this task. Such an international group was founded in 1956, inspired by Roberto Assagioli and Foster Bailey (the husband of Alice A. Bailey), and Michal Eastcott was one of the pioneers. An example of this work is Meditation Mount in the Ojai Valley in California, USA, where a group of disciples for years have been meeting every morning at 9 a.m. in order to meditate on the 6 laws and principles in relation to the events of the world.

These laws and principles are divided in pairs among the 3 aspects which are emphasized so distinctly by the esoteric teaching. The principles are basic mechanisms in the spiritual worlds of the higher self, and the laws are tools by which the principles are realized in the 3 worlds of the personality:

*1st Aspect*: The Principle of Essential Divinity & The Law of Spiritual Approach.
*2nd Aspect*: The Principle of Goodwill & The Law of Right Human Relations.
*3rd Aspect*: The Principle of Unanimity & The Law of Group Endeavour.

But, as mentioned above, generally the creative meditation is used for personality growth, and therefore we will give an example. The meditation aims at creating a realistic ideal which we may substitute for the incoherent image we usually have of ourselves. This requires that we become aware of the various aspects of the self-image which limit our anticipation of what we may become.

## Creative Meditation

Relax the body, and perform a quick alignment. Concentrate on the image you have of yourself, and reflect exhaustively on its various aspects.

- There are aspects of your self-image where you underestimate yourself. Notice how you feel in relation to them.
- There are also aspects of your self-image where you overestimate yourself. Again, be aware of how you feel about them.
- There is a part of your self-image which shows how you would like to be. This is an entirely unrealistic daydream which is unproductive and stands in the way of a realistic perception.
- There is an aspect which shows how you would like to appear to others – in contrast to how you really are.
- The thoughtform which constitutes your self-image is also influenced by projections from other people in regard to how they perceive you.
- And finally, your self-image contains a portrayal of how other people want you to be, what they expect from you, and what they want to change.

Try to form an overview of these images put together, and realize how they limit you and keep you down. Gather all your inner strength, and imagine that you shake them off with one powerful act of will. Be quiet for a moment and observe your emotions.

Now, return to the centre of your being, and visualize what you really and realistically would like to be. Let the image grow out of the experiences you have just had.

Finally, visualize yourself as if you already were this truthful and realistic self-image. See yourself in different situations in everyday life and make the decision that you want to bring this self-image into being.[1]

## The Method of Meditation

Because many people think that the most important issue is to create "emptiness" in consciousness during meditation, they also think that the first thing we do is to eliminate the brain function. They sit down and wait for a direct connection with "God", and they expect it to happen by itself – something "God" fixes. But it is quite the reversed situation.

Meditation begins with an intense concentration in the brain, for it is in the brain consciousness that we decide to meditate and sit down to begin. And because of the tendency of the brain-mind to be restless, there is usually a very demanding thought and visualization activity in the beginning of the meditation in order to overcome this tendency.

As this activity proceeds consciousness slides imperceptibly into the mental body while the brain is kept open and receptive. This is experienced as an increasing clarity and depth of thought. Sometimes it leads to a sensation which may be illustrated by the image of flying a kite. In the beginning, we stand firmly on the ground, holding the string with the brain consciousness while the kite is something distant, hovering high above us in the air. But gradually, we glide upwards along the string, ending up as the kite on the

[1] Reprinted in Psychosynthesis Practice, Vol. 1, p. 25.

mental plane looking down at the man on the ground holding the string. Up here, we sense the whistling of the air and the wind and we experience a freedom entirely unknown in the physical world – even if it is really the brain consciousness which is reflecting it.

Emotional reactions are deliberately cut off. This is not difficult if we really lose ourselves in the process and concentrate on the work – and not merely the result. The emotions can only be a hindrance if they have already been stirred before we begin meditating. In that case, we simply have to wait until the emotional body is sufficiently quiet and serene to permit us to concentrate. It may take a while, and sometimes we never get to meditate that day as it may take as long as 48 hours for the emotional body to quiet down after a violent outburst of rage. That is why it is wise not to look to any of the sides when you get up in the morning. Wear blinkers to the bathroom, take a shower in order to wake up (and become clean, of course), and then move directly toward the meditation chair which has been "vibrated" into the right "frequency" for many years.

We don't have to feel good when we meditate. But of course, we shouldn't feel bad either. We shouldn't feel at all, for it consumes energy which might otherwise be available for the meditation process itself. This is where visualization is so important, for as it is based on the imagination – which is an astral quality – and at the same time directed by the will during meditation, it means that the entire desire function is lifted up to the highest sphere of the astral world and only permitted to express itself as aspiration. And our aspiration is not liable to disturb the process, for it knows very well what meditation means for the spiritual development it desires.

During all this process, the mind is driven to the utmost of its capacity until it finally reaches its own limit. It is like driving a dog in front of yourself until it is captured in a corner from where it cannot escape. It gasps for air, and for a brief moment it stops completely after the heavy strain, and the same thing may happen to the mind during meditation. After the tiring effort, there is a small vacuum, and as nature does not accept vacua it must be filled up immediately. The question is from where? If consciousness has cut off impulses from "below", that is, the brain and the emotional body, and from "outside", the mental surroundings, it can only be filled from "above", that is, the soul and the higher self. This is what the whole process of meditation is all about, whether it is a meditation with or without a seed thought.

Here the effort of the personality stops, for we cannot force our entrance into the dimension of the soul. We can only remove the hindrances, create the right conditions, and then hope for the best. This is done by the intensity of the meditation effort, for afterwards there is a natural standstill, just as there is a natural relaxation of the muscles after heavy physical strain.

But it is evident from the above that the whole thing depends on the state of mental tension which is established during the meditation. And this is where most people are mistaken in their expectations. The power reserve needed in the inner dimensions to really contact the soul in its own world is not present in the life of the aspirant before he has taken what is esoterically termed the 2$^{nd}$ initiation and is very close to the 3$^{rd}$ initiation. For it means that the "organ" of the spiritual will, the so-called "atmic" body, has to be formed so that it may supply the extra dynamism which is needed, and this formation happens around the 2$^{nd}$ initiation.

## Contemplation

If these conditions are met with and the vacuum in consciousness is filled by the soul or higher self, it means that the disciple stands in the world of the soul itself. He enters into the higher mental sphere and is consciously present in the world of ideas and causes. The mind and the brain are open to impressions but do not interfere with their own processes.

We are told that the dimensional difference is so great that it is impossible to describe the state of consciousness in words. We may only hint at the experiences which are portrayed in esoteric books where the condition is often termed "contemplation" or "samadhi".

It is a complete liberation from the 3 worlds of the personality – that is, sense perception, desire, and analytical thinking – and it means that all of manifestation is seen as light. At the same time, there is such an identification with the consciousness of the soul that the aspirant becomes aware of the soul in everything. He may look out into the world of the soul in the same way that he can look out on the physical plane with his eyes.

The contemplating unit of consciousness is present in what is termed the "universal mind".[1] Here it witnesses the activities which govern the planetary life and is able to "read" what the Indian yogi Patanjali called the "rain cloud of knowable things" – that is, the collected amount of "information" the planetary Logos has embodied in the evolution on that plane.

In that dimension, there is an experience of unity with all souls, and the ability to communicate telepathically with them. The personal identity is no longer the pivot of everything but is seen solely as an instrument by which the soul can communicate with the 3 lower worlds.[2]

For millions of years, the incarnated soul has been completely identified with the forms in the 3 worlds, and has only visited its own dimension between incarnations. Now, suddenly, it is consciously present there at the same time as it is incarnated. Naturally, it is merely occasional glimpses in the beginning, but as the "thread" which connects the outer and inner worlds is spun there are longer periods of soul contact.

The experience is said to be completely unforgettable – the aspirant is never the same again. But at the same time, there is the sense that he should not speak about it to others, unless he is absolutely certain that they have attained the same or a higher level of evolution than himself.

If he offends against this rule he runs the risk of giving rise to cynical remarks from people who are envious of his experiences, or he may bring about an authoritarian worship of himself by people who admire him – and it is difficult to say which of the 2 alternatives is the worst. But anyway, we may draw the conclusion that

[1] *Universal Mind*: The cosmic physical thought processes of the planetary Logos. *Logos*: Greek for "word" or "thought", the cosmic intelligence of the planet corresponding to the biblical "God".

[2] Alice A. Bailey: The Light of the Soul, p. 250 – edited & adapted.

those who go about telling others of their sublime contact with the soul are the very people who have not had such experiences.

## Illumination

Here we should realize what it is that is being illuminated. It is not the soul, for this is the being who illuminates. So, it is the mind and the brain, and that is why on Figure 5 (page 35) we depicted the meditation process as an arc with an "ascent" and a "descent". Alignment, dedication, and meditation is the ascent, contemplation is the turning point, while illumination, realization, and service are the descent.

So, by illumination we mean that the soul projects its "light" down into the personality – always remembering that "light" stands for insight and understanding. When we say "throwing light" on a subject we really mean bring about clarity of understanding. The mind receives the light and creates thoughtforms, while the brain formulates the forms in language and directs the realization.

Alice A. Bailey says that the effect on the mental body is a direct perception of universal knowledge which is quite impersonal and does not raise any questions – that is, it is experienced as infallible. Moreover, there is the ability to contact other disciples on a corresponding evolutionary level telepathically.

The effect on the emotional body is a neutralization of all fear and worry. They are replaced by a "peace that passeth understanding" – as it is expressed in the First Ray Blessing. It is a euphoric bliss, but like all other emotions it is ephemeral.

The effect on the physical body is a stimulation to a flurry of activity. The person in question talks and writes with a feverish intensity which drains away the vitality and may in the long run shatter the nervous system if the aspirant is not careful – that is, making sure that he sleeps sufficiently and takes some time off when the pressure gets too high.

To this must be added the registration of what is called the "light in the head", an etheric light which is due to the fact that the "voltage" between the brow centre, where the personality forces are focused, and the head centre, where the energies of the soul enter the organism, is so high that a "spark" is drawn between the 2 points, lightening the halo. In the beginning, it is experienced as a blurred light outside and around the head – especially in the evening just before one falls asleep. Later it is focused within the head as a large blinding sun, and finally an electric blue point arises in the centre of the sphere and a golden path shoots out, symbolizing the path of evolution.

How much the aspirant is able to perceive depends on the development of the physical-etheric sense mechanism. Some people are very sensitive and see it all almost at once while others never experience more than a vague feeling. But this does not concern their spiritual status. A person may very well have the light in the head without being aware of it. As a matter of fact, this is the most common situation.

The whole of the process has a healing effect on neurotic and other psychological symptoms. This is due to the fact that all aspects of the consciousness are illuminated – also those which are otherwise hidden because of blocking or repression.

Generally, we may say that as an aspirant is pressing his awareness higher and higher into the spiritual regions, parts of the subconscious content is surfacing with it in order to be deliberately integrated with the rest of the consciousness. For when he reaches the end of the cycle of human evolution, by the stage which is technically termed the 4th initiation, all functions of consciousness must be purified and integrated with the total consciousness. And as we have seen above, consciousness is always tied up with forms of substance because it is the result of the meeting of life energy and substance or matter, and since the 4th initiation is the final "goodbye" to all substance in the 3 worlds of human existence there cannot be any "unredeemed" residue left.

At the same time, the disciple has the advantage of being able to see his subconscious responses in a larger and more enlightened perspective, so that he may relatively easy resolve the tension and integrate the material, while other people with more deep-seated neurotic symptoms have to fight them "face to face" – if we may use such an expression.

## Realization and Service

The impressions from the meditation are converted into a plan of action by the physical consciousness, and thus they are channeled into the service work. We have seen that in relation to historical figures like the Buddha, Krishna, the Christ, or Mohammed. They are all expressions of the path of spiritual evolution, resting on 3 disciplines: meditation, study, and service.

Everybody who has tried to tread this path recognize that the perception of the world becomes somewhat simpler and at the same time deeper in such a way that it evades a description with physical means of communication.

We know from the esoteric teaching that at the root of the system lies one single energy, namely, "life" or "spirit" – which are synonymous terms. But how this energy ramifies into the amazing variety we know from the physical world is entirely beyond the incarnated consciousness.

We find the same principle in messages from the great founders of religions. Very often, they are incredibly simple, so simple that it is difficult to understand them, because everything depends on the practical realization of them. For instance, the Buddha says something like: desire is the root of all suffering – stop desiring! Such a statement is very difficult to understand for people, who have not yet caught the sight of their own desire function, and, therefore, are entirely unable to realize it.

In the same way, the Christ says that God is love, and that this love is latent in all people and realized through service. It may be difficult to grasp what he means when we look at the physical world and ascertain the amount of suffering going on here. It really takes a deep philosophical insight to relate to statements of that kind, an insight that – if we follow it to the end – would imply knowledge of the concepts which the esoteric teaching presents.

# Invocation and Evocation

After the appearance of the modern esoteric teaching, two relatively new concepts have been introduced into occult meditation, namely, "invocation" and "evocation".

Invocation means to "call upon", and it has to a certain degree replaced prayer among esoterically inclined people. Prayer has been a general characteristic of the Christian era and may be divided into 4 groups:

1. Prayer for material welfare or help.
2. Prayer for virtues – that is, qualities of character.
3. Prayer for others – that is, intercession.
4. Prayer for enlightenment and divine insight.[1]

The difference between them is that prayer is based on a state of emotion where from our desperate situation we appeal to higher powers for help, while invocation combines all the elements of consciousness in the following way:

- *Prayerful attitude of the heart* –
  magnetic appeal based on emotional devotion.
- *Meditative action of the mind* –
  assertion of a rightful demand based on a mental understanding of the lawfulness of the inner worlds.
- *Focused will or intention* –
  the power of expectation based on the conviction that the good will conquer.[2]

When we invoke we are sure that help will be the outcome if we are sufficiently focused. This is what is termed "evocation", which means "call forth". Therefore, we may say that we really do both things ourselves. First, we invoke, and thereby we also evoke because the whole of the process is lawful, that is, the powers who help us cannot refuse if the invocation is done in the right way and

[1] Alice A. Bailey: *From Intellect to Intuition*, p. 67 – edited & adapted.
[2] Michal Eastcott: *The Silent Path*, pp. 119-120 – edited & adapted.

with the right motive. What we don't know is which form the help will take, and when it is brought about. This depends on the plan of evolution and karma.[1]

So, evocation is the lawful result of invocation, and the two together may be seen as a modern formulation of the biblical statement:

> *"Ask, and it shall be given you; seek, and ye shall find; knock, and it shall be opened unto you: For every one that asketh receiveth; and he that seeketh findeth; and to him that knocketh it shall be opened".*[2]

Just as prayer was the heart of the Christian religion, invocation and evocation will be the primary foundation for the new world religion. This is not because the method is new and wasn't known before, but because humanity has only recently qualified itself for the use of it by learning to think.

After the victory of the forces of light in the second World War, the Tibetan released through Alice A. Bailey a very powerful invocation called *The Great Invocation,* and we are told that it is going to replace the *Lord's Prayer* as the primary approach to the divine. It is simple and clear, and it conveys some basic truths which all people with some degree of spiritual affinity may accept, irrespective of what religion or philosophy they otherwise adhere to. And the Tibetan tells us that it is not only used by humanity to invoke the Hierarchy but also by members of the Hierarchy to invoke Shamballa.[3]

[1] *Karma*: The law of cause and effect, action and reaction.

[2] Matthew 7:7.

[3] *Shamballa*: The crown centre or highest spiritual focal point of the earth.

# The Creative Word

*"There is a word which expresses perfectly the true Self, the Soul of everything that lives. That word, when spoken with understanding, produces a sound which is creative. It will create the form through control of the vibration of substance into which a thought is made manifest, thus giving it the proper clothing for its appearance in the light of day… That word is very simple, being composed of just two letters: 'OM'".*[1]

After this statement, we are asked to do a brief exercise in order to ascertain for ourselves the reality of what is said in the above quotation. The exercise simply consists in saying:

*I am a conscious Soul incarnate… OM*

Perhaps we may here begin to understand why the creative word, "OM", is so widely used in occult meditation, but in order to get a clearer picture we will take a look at the effect of sound in general terms.

Sound is a creative agent, for the worlds we live in "are the effect of sound", as the Tibetan says. Sound sets into motion the substance of which all forms are made. It may increase, decrease, or even change the direction of the motion it already has, but it always has an effect – according to its frequency.

Naturally, the word "sound" should be understood in a figurative sense, owing to the fact that these creative processes take place in dimensions we are quite unable to relate to. So, maybe it is better to say that the system is created by the type of force or vibration which we would call sound in the physical world.

In a deeply metaphysical sense we may say that sound is the medium which connects. It is the creative intermediate link in the process of manifestation, the linking third factor which is occultly termed "the relation between".

The Tibetan says about using the sacred word in connection with meditation:

[1] Lucille Cedercrans: *The Path of Initiation – Volume I,* Lesson 9, Speech.

> *"In the sounding of the Sacred Word in meditation man should (if rightly sounding it forth) be able to do both the creative work and the destructive work... He will attract to his bodies matter of the finer kind and cast out that which is coarser. He will formulate thoughtforms that attract to themselves finer matter and repudiate that which is of a lower vibration. He should so sound the Word that alignment will be automatically made, and the necessary vacuum created, eventuating in a downflow from above. All these effects can transpire when the Word is correctly intoned, and each meditation should see the man more aligned, should disperse some of the matter of low vibration in one or other of his bodies, should open up the channel to a greater extent, and so provide a more adequate vehicle for the illumination from higher levels".*[1]

Therefore, it is often used in relation to the alignment or coordination of the bodies in the beginning of the meditation where it is pronounced 3 times:

- First time gently and in relation to the mental body.
- Second time a little louder and in relation to the emotional body.
- Third time still louder and in relation to the physical body.

This has the following effects:

On the mental body:
- It is calming the lower mind.
- It establishes contact with the soul in the egoic lotus.[2]
- It expels coarse particles and builds in finer ones.

On the emotional body:
- It stabilizes the emotional nature and activates the heart centre.
- It drives out coarse particles and makes the vehicle more colorless so that it is able to reflect higher frequencies.

[1] Alice A. Bailey: *Letters on Occult Meditation*, pp. 58-59.
[2] *Egoic lotus*: The golden 12-petalled lotus of the soul in its own world.

- It establishes a connection from the highest, that is, atomic, subplane[1] to the buddhic plane via the atomic channel[2] which exists between the planes.

On the physical body:

- It purifies and clarifies primarily the etheric body and stimulates the energy flow.
- It creates a shell around the body, protecting it and driving away disturbing influences in the vicinity.[3]

But naturally, we should be aware of the fact that it may be exceedingly difficult – amounting almost to impossible – to pronounce the word in such a way that it has the effects described above.

Now we have introduced all the elements of occult meditation, including invocation, evocation, and the use of the creative word, so therefore we will present a meditation which is a far more complete demonstration of this form of meditation – with The Great Invocation as a natural closing.

## Occult Meditation

***Introduction***

Settle yourself comfortably, relax the body, straighten the back, and close your eyes. Rest your arms and legs in a natural way, take a deep breath, and then forget all about the breath.

[1] *Subplane*: Each plane is divided into 7 subplanes according to the frequency or "size" of "particles".

[2] *Atomic channel*: Arises out of the structure of the atoms of the various planes. They all represent spiral movements built into each other like a Chinese nest of boxes, so that there is a direct connection from an atom of a plane to the atoms of the planes above through its internal structure.

[3] Alice A. Bailey: *Letters on Occult Meditation*, pp. 62-63 – edited & adapted.

Raise your consciousness to the middle of the head – a point abreast of the brow. This is the ordinary brain consciousness. Imagine that the light of the soul flows down through the top of the head and merges with the consciousness behind the brow. Project the light further down into the region of the heart between the shoulder blades and light the "sun" of the soul in your heart. (This is merely fleeting images and not a direct focus in the heart centre.)

*Alignment*

Say in your mind: *On the ray of the mental body solar fire pervades my mind and purifies my thoughts and conceptions.* Imagine how the "sunbeams" from the heart flow out into the coloured, egg shaped bubble, which is your mental body, and purify and illuminate it.

Say in your mind: *On the ray of the astral body solar fire pervades my emotional nature and purifies my feelings and desires*. Imagine a corresponding process in a slightly smaller egg shape which is your emotional body.

Say in your mind: *On the ray of the physical body solar fire pervades my vital body and purifies my etheric network.* See how the "sunbeams" cleanse and illuminate the subtle, moonlight-colored etheric channels which form a network that permeates the dense body and stretches a couple of centimetres outside of it.

*Dedication*

Imagine a path of golden light, leading from where you stand to a vast two-leaved door (the path and door of initiation).

Then see, rolling along this path, a sphere of rose (unselfish love), which you send forth and which eventually disappears through the door.

Then send along the same track a sphere of vivid green (sympathy and compassion), and see it disappear the same way.

Then send a sphere of a radiant, electric blue (spiritual aspiration and idealism), which rolls along the golden Path but which does not enter the door but remains there, hiding the door from sight.

Picture then yourself as standing before the electric blue sphere, saying in your mind:

*I stand in spiritual Being and, as a soul, I serve.*
*I stand within the Light, and as the light shines throughout my form, I radiate that light.*
*I stand within the love of God, and as that love streams through and from the heart, I magnetize the ones I seek to aid.*[1]

Send out from your heart, via the brow, the light and love of your soul to all those who suffer in the world. It may be family, friends (say their names), groups of persons or humanity as a whole.

***Meditation***

Hold your consciousness in the light of the head and meditate on the following seed thought:

*I am the Way myself, the door am I. I am the golden Path and in the light of my own light I tread the Way: I enter through the door. I turn and radiate.*[2]

Think about the seed thought from all "angles". What does it mean that I am the way and the door? What is my own light? Why do I turn and radiate? And many other questions and associations.

[1] Alice A. Bailey: *Discipleship in the New Age I*, p. 213 – edited & adapted.
[2] *Ibid.*, p. 303.

***Conclusion***

Conclude by saying The Great Invocation. Visualize each stanza when you say it, and see how the energies of light, love, and power envelop the earth, restoring and renewing all aspects of its life and existence:

*From the point of Light within the Mind of God*
*Let light stream forth into the minds of men.*
*Let Light descend on Earth.*

*From the point of Love within the Heart of God*
*Let love stream forth into the hearts of men.*
*May Christ return to Earth.*

*From the center where the Will of God is known*
*Let purpose guide the little wills of men –*
*The purpose which the Masters know and serve.*

*From the center which we call the race of men*
*Let the Plan of Love and Light work out*
*And may it seal the door where evil dwells.*

*Let Light and Love and Power*
*restore the Plan on earth.*

*OM… OM… OM…*

# The Practical Work

Let us begin this section by quoting a very wise man. The Lord Buddha said:

> *"It were better to live one single day in the pursuit of understanding and meditation than to live a hundred years in ignorance and unrestraint".*[1]

This is really a very pragmatic statement for it invites us to begin right away – now! Therefore, we will have a look at the many practical aspects of the meditation work.

## Place

We should have a definite place to meditate, although it may be difficult to find in modern family life. But we must be sure that we are not disturbed, for if we are anxious that this may happen it spoils the concentration.

If there is no vacant room available we have to get up earlier in the morning and use a corner of the living room. Here we may place a few symbolic things which convey the atmosphere we need. If even this isn't feasible we may turn down a quiet residential street on the way to work and meditate in the car. And ultimately, we might find a "secluded" corner at the workplace as for instance sitting on the floor in one of the rest rooms and meditate. Naturally, the latter two alternatives are not very good, but basically they are better than nothing because they demonstrate the persistence which is necessary.

But of course, it is best to have a fixed and undisturbed place which we can use every time. If that is the case and nobody else is using it we will soon build a protective shell around it which makes it easier to contact the higher dimensions. The surrounding substance becomes attuned to a certain vibration – which is the highest

[1] Michal Eastcott: *The Silent Path*, p. IX.

the meditator is able to reach – and that makes it easier to start on that level next time.

Some people may try to meditate in beautiful surroundings from the idea that having an aesthetic experience might contribute to raising the level of consciousness. But here we should remember that consciousness moves inward during meditation, so that outer beauty may become a distraction if we are aware of it.

It goes without saying that music or any other form of sound is an even greater distraction. This is also true of the other types of sense impressions as for instance meditating with open eyes, feeling something touching us, sucking a sweet, or smelling something – with the exception of burning incense which may have a beneficial effect if it isn't overdone. Every sense impression will keep some part of the consciousness tied to the brain.

So, it is clear that the important thing is to cut off all of the sensory apparatus as much as possible. If there are loud noises coming from the neighbour, maybe earplugs are the solution, even if it takes a while to get used to the feeling. But out of two evils, it is always wise to choose the lesser one, and we should especially be aware of the possibility that outer disturbances may become an excuse for not meditating. Where there is a will there is also a way.

## Time

It is wise to meditate within the same space of time every day, although this may also be difficult to accomplish in modern family life. It is our personal choice to meditate, and therefore it should not be a burden to the other members of the family – neither directly (quiet, daddy meditates!) nor indirectly (I am better than you because I meditate!)

The best time is in the morning where consciousness is fresh and "pristine", that is, after the shower so we are quite awake, but before breakfast because it takes energy to digest the food. At the same time, it is wise to stay neutral when we wake up after a night's sleep and not start to make plans for the day. For if we are neutral and find ourselves in a sort of no man's land between sleep and the activities of the day, it is the soul who sets the agenda during the meditation, and not the personality before the meditation.

But if it is impossible to meditate in the morning we have to find another space of time and then try to make it the same interval every day.

## Rhythm

The crucial factor is regularity. This implies habit and is called "rhythm". Once the habit is established we don't have to decide whether we are going to meditate or not. We become agitated and get a bad conscience if we do not meditate. Such a habit gradually turns the whole of the personality focus inwards and upwards toward the soul.

## Posture

It is important to sit comfortably so that the body does not require attention. But the position should not be so comfortable that we fall asleep. The back must be upright – this supports the upward orientation of consciousness. The head should be balanced. It is usually heavier than we think so that it takes a lot of strength to carry it in a wrong position. Arms and legs should rest in a natural way, and many find it best to fold their hands in the lap and cross the ankles. This circulates the body forces and makes it easier to concentrate.

A natural position soon becomes a habit and thereby supports the processes of consciousness which are connected to it – according to Roberto Assagioli's psychological law No. 2, which says that *attitudes, movements, and actions tend to evoke corresponding images and ideas.*[1] The subconscious simply learns that when we assume the position meditation follows.

But from then on, all activities must be conscious, and the first conscious action is relaxation. For instance, concentration will often

[1] Roberto Assagioli: *The Act of Will*, p. 52.

cause us to knit our brows, clench our fists, or set our teeth, and that disturbs the concentration because actions begin as thoughtforms in the mental body and are projected from there into the physical organism. Therefore, an action, performed as a muscular tension, is associated with the mind and ties up some part of our consciousness – again according to Assagioli's psychological law No. 2. So, we should remember areas where we are subconsciously liable to flex the muscles, such as the scalp, eyes, eyelids, tongue, and other parts of the musculature.

## Breath

It is usually wise to slow down the rhythm of breathing by making it deeper. This calms the organism and tells it that there is no danger. For when we are in danger we usually get short of breath, and that is just the opposite. The experience of danger is a state of emotion, and when we tell the organism that there is no danger we also calm our emotions and thoughts.

This is not what is normally considered breathing exercises. These come into the picture at a far more advanced stage of development, partly because they may be dangerous, and partly because it requires experience to utilize the techniques. All that is needed is a quiet breathing rhythm which can be used to calm the body, emotions and mind. This may be done by counting during inhaling and exhaling, but not to the extent that it becomes a predominant activity which attracts mental awareness. So, as soon as the breath is quiet we stop counting.

# Evening Review

The daily rhythm of meditation is not complete until another discipline is added to the morning meditation, namely, the evening review. As the designation suggests, it consists in looking back over the day when it is finished, that is, at some time in the evening.

The intention is to assume the position of the soul as the observer of the life of the personality so that we may keep an eye on the character deficiencies we try to remedy. This stabilizes the anchoring of consciousness in the soul nature, which the whole of the meditation project tries to establish, for the soul is the Archimedean point which makes it possible for the personality to alter its character.

By assuming the observing attitude of the soul we use a technique often recommended in esoteric psychology: the "as-if technique". We imagine that we really are the soul and are able to look impersonally back on the events of the day, for energy follows thought, and when we act as the soul we stimulate the process, which will eventually transform us into a soul, expressing itself in the dimensions of the personality.

Actually, the transformation that spiritual development results in – if genuine – is very gradual, so that it may be difficult to determine exactly whether the qualities we seek to unfold are really beginning to gain a footing in the personality, or the notion of being something we are not dominates. But naturally, we should avoid posing for our fellow human beings and pretend that we already have the qualities we are trying to develop.

The as-if technique is a quiet inner process where a person consciously regulates the sum of reactions which dominate the inner state of consciousness and surfaces as behaviour. We always face a number of possible reactions to all that happens. This is due to the fact that the bodies – with their content of elemental essences – have their own instinctive consciousness which at any time produces the reaction that suits the "elemental"[1] best at that particular time. Simultaneously, the consciousness of the soul tries to express itself through the bodies, and the meeting of these two very diffe-

[1] *Elemental*: Designation of the total amount of elemental essence in a body. It often appears as a "whole" being because the tendencies of the individual parts are the same.

rent streams of consciousness results in our collective state, minute by minute of the day.

Therefore, we may say that we, when we use the as-if technique, try to distance ourselves and ignore the impulses from the elementals of the various bodies and focus on the part of the consciousness produced by the presence of soul instead. In this way, the technique becomes a concrete approach to the soul, and the only pretentious part of it is that it is not as stable as it would be, if we were able to eliminate the influence of the elemental essence entirely.

Let us take an example. We are in the situation where we have lost one of our loved ones. A natural reaction would be deep sorrow. This will primarily arise from the emotional elemental "who" is interested in "heavy" vibrations like that. But we might also try to emphasize the more mental conception of the situation and understand that the deceased is in a happy and liberated state, and that the grief therefore primarily concerns our personal loss and is a sort of self-pity. So, the lack of sorrow in that situation is not necessarily an expression of truncated cynicism, but may be due to the fact that the soul in a person has such power as to lead the consciousness into sublime states as that of accompanying the dead on his way in the next dimension – corresponding to what people in other contexts try to do by "reading to the dead".

In many ways, it is the "as-if technique" which has brought the whole status of humanity forward characterwise and morally down through the ages, even if the motive has always been mixed. It may be that people with questionable morals still seek to keep within the law because of fear from being in conflict with the minions of the law. It may also be younger people who suddenly take an interest in the elder generation to be sure that they get a prominent position in the will. But it may just be people who change their thoughts, feelings, and actions in the attempt to live up to idols like the Buddha, the Christ, or Mohammed, and in those situations the process is extremely valuable and may very well be compared to modern, esoteric use of the as-if technique.

## The Review Itself

Normally, the best time for the review is in the evening just before we go to bed so that we include as much of the day as possible. But of course we should also be awake and concentrated, and if this is a problem we may choose another time and just see to it that it is approximately the same each day. A day and night has 24 hours, and fundamentally the review may be placed at any time as long as the remaining part of the day and evening enters into the review of the next day. But as we remember clearest the same day we look back on, most people choose to place the review in the evening.

The optimal way in which to do the review is going through the day backwards so that we begin with the evening and end with the morning. This makes it easier to observe the events at a "distance", with the eyes of the spectator instead of reliving them and identifying with them. But as always, if it is a problem to do so we simply turn around and remember forwards, beginning with the morning and ending with the evening.

During the review, it is important to stay as impersonal as possible, and this is easiest to do if we clearly, quietly, and relatively quickly register every phase. It is not the intention that we should relive the day in order to criticize, downrate, condemn, defend, or praise ourselves. First of all, we are trying to penetrate into the meaning of the events and the motives of our reactions so that we get a realistic picture of whom and what we really are. And we always remember the motto that "we are human and nothing human is foreign to us" – that is, we are ready to forgive ourselves any trait we may discover during the review in the light of the soul.

The whole of the meditation project is about changing ourselves and the world we live in for the better, and we are not able to change anything we don't know how works. Imagine that we are presented with the task of rebuilding a huge and complicated machine without a manual on the structure and function of the machine. Where shall we begin and with what? And we humans are probably the most complicated "devices" which have ever been brought into the world, so here it is utmost important that if we want to change our nature we must have an intimate knowledge of it – not as we think, hope, or guess that it is, but as it *really* is. Here the review is a great help.

Naturally, this may be done in various ways. One of these is to see oneself and one's existence as a whole, and here it is wise to use different angles of view at the same time to secure the greatest possible degree of impersonality. We may for instance imagine (1) how a "Master" would estimate the efforts of the day, (2) how the surroundings have reacted to that which we said and did, and (3) how we ourselves understand the meaning of the events and the motives for our behaviour.

Another method consists in focusing on the various subpersonalities we are composed of. Often, these operate fairly independent of each other and know in many cases nothing of the existence of the others. Some of them are personal and typical for the individual while others are shared by many people, such as the "child", the "seeker", the "clinger", or the "poet". Therefore, it may be a rather uncertain designation when ordinarily we say "I" about ourselves – which "I"? If we for instance observe our likes and dislikes we find that one moment we like one thing and the next moment another thing, and those things are so different in nature that it is obvious that the two "I's", who each like his own thing, never meet.

The same goes for our decisions. One "I" may make a decision which another "I" has to put into practice. But this other "I" may be very reluctant to do so – provided it has heard of any decision in the first place. For instance, we decide to get up early in the morning, but the "I" who is getting up next morning is liable to find all sorts of excuses to stay in bed a little longer. In extreme situations, this mechanism may have very unpleasant consequences. If a random "I" in a romantic and optimistic moment signs a mortgage deed, other "I's" will have to suffer for it the rest of the person's life.

Here we begin to understand what is meant by the esoteric expression "to integrate[1] the personality". It simply means to reduce these many "I's" and roles to one single identity under the direction of the mind, but such a unifying activity can only come from the

[1] *Integrate*: To "make whole".

soul. So, it is the inspiration from the soul which brings about the integration of the personality, and therefore we may say that as long as the soul has not really started to align and direct the personality, it necessarily consists of many different "I's", roles, or masks – primarily produced by the changeable desire function. But the problem is that we do not really notice it because all the time we are identified with the latest "I" and consider it to be the whole of the "I".

At the same time, there is a definite psychological mechanism which prevents us from noticing the passage from one "I" to another. The cause of this is the many conflicting opinions, emotions, and notions we have placed all about the various subpersonalities. If we were to be conscious of all these contradictions we would live in a constant state of tension. We would become insane by experiencing ourselves the sport of fleeting moods, and we would completely lose our self-confidence and self-esteem which are based on the illusion of unity, vigor, courage, and strength.

So, in this situation there are only two possibilities: either to eradicate the contradictions by establishing a still closer contact with the soul through meditation, or stop noticing the contradictions, and this is where the psychological mechanism comes into the picture.

For instance, we adopt the position about ourselves that we are never jealous. This is our opinion about ourselves in that respect, and we support it by explanations about how irrational it is to think that we can own each other, that it is necessary to have freedom if we are going to progress, and that it is unreasonable that our spouses cannot have fun with other people, etc. – completely ignoring the fact that jealousy has nothing to do with the rational mind but arises in the deeper layers of the emotional nature and enters physical consciousness through the lower centers. Then we may be as jealous as we want, for while we are actually jealous we are unable to observe ourselves, and if we ask ourselves if we are jealous we get the answer that we never are.

This mechanism is termed "rationalization", and the function of it is that our vanity will not admit that we are jealous like everybody else, and therefore asks the intellect to present an explanation which sounds probable and at the same time explains away the phenomenon. The emotion engages the mind as its lawyer, and as it is not the mind who is vain, but the personality working through the emotions, we succeed in preventing the two aspects from meeting each other and discover the reality.

Therefore, it may be wise during the evening review to focus on one's subpersonalities, and in this connection it is profitable, before one does the review for the first time, to take a look at oneself and try to register which subpersonalities are the most active and typical for us at the time.

But let us try out a concrete illustration of how an evening review is. Many people find it valuable to first write down the psychological observations they make. Then they may later evaluate if there are definite patterns which are repeated but difficult to spot if they don't have a statistical overview. Secondly, they may gradually establish a sort of psychological journal which is always valuable to have if they are working with themselves in a serious and persevering way. Many things in the life of the aspirant depend on whether he knows himself or not.

### Evening Review

In this review, you look back at the day from the 3 primary aspects of the personality: the physical consciousness, the emotional nature, and the mind or intellect.

You ask yourself the following questions:

1. Which aspect was I identified with most of the time?
2. Which different subpersonalities were prominent at different times during the day? What circumstances (inner or outer) made them come forward or recede?
3. Which valuable qualities or which limitations did they possess individually? Did they help me, or did they stand in the way for me?

4. What did each subpersonality want? What did it want my life to be if it could decide?
5. Was there a conflict between some of them?
6. Were my subpersonalities in harmony with what I wanted, or did I have to yield to them?
7. What role did I play in regard to reconciling and directing them?[1]

[1] Psychosynthesis Practice, Vol. 1, p. 9.

# Group Meditation

## Introduction

Even if meditation in most cases begins as an individual activity, it often happens – as within other areas of activity – that we become part of a greater whole which gives us a sense of meaning and purpose. Through meditation we enter into states of consciousness which other people also take part in, and in this way we find a companionship which we have never experienced before.

Concurrently, we live in a time where there is a world-wide tendency to perform tasks in groups. Everywhere in the economic life, state, municipalities, and educational institutions, groups are formed in order to solve problems. Perhaps the groups are called committees, but the effect is the same.

Fundamentally, this tendency arises in a change of the "energy climate" which influences everything that happens on earth. Here are 2 factors of special significance: (1) the zodiacal sign, Aquarius, we are entering into in the shorter cycle of about 2,500 years, and (2) the ray which is particularly dominating evolution in the coming cycle – namely, the 7th ray of order, organization, and physical manifestation.

But as the cyclical influence of these energies on the evolution of earth is directed by that which is somewhat misleadingly called "The Inner Government of the World" or "The Hierarchy", we are not surprised that the tendency to group work is especially prevalent in esoteric service work which is the consequence of the appearance of the modern esoteric teaching in the last 125 years. The teaching tells us that the group tendency is so strong that spiritual development no longer takes place on the individual level but only in groups. This is expressed by Lucille Cedercrans with the words:

> *"The whole time this has been going on in one individual it has been going on in the group of individuals, for growth cannot proceed for only the one. It is group relationship, group reaction, group solving that is working out through this magnetic field. One lifts the other in consciousness until the door is opened for all as a group to proceed through the open door of understanding, wisdom and light... The*

*Soul is group conscious. It is impossible to become a conscious Soul incarnate as an individual. The conscious Soul can only incarnate in a group instrumentality".*[1]

Even initiation, which was formerly a distinctly individual phenomenon, is today taken in groups. This means that when occult meditation is the primary tool of development the concept of "individual meditation" will gradually die out and be replaced by group meditation.

But there is also another and perhaps more "distant" cause of the tendency of the times to bring about synthesis, fusion, unity, and group formation. It is that the whole of the evolutionary process ultimately approaches the planetary group consciousness which is the only natural expression of the fact that all which happens on the planet is merely local processes in the evolution of consciousness of a single cosmic being – the being esoterically termed the planetary Logos.

Evolution has for millions of years been focused on the development of the qualities of individual man. It is not because this has been the "best" solution to the "problems" of evolution, but because it has been the only possibility, considering the starting point of human consciousness – that is, total self-absorbed egoism.

But for some time past, the evolution of consciousness has progressed with great rapidity. This has primarily shown itself in the explosive development of the human intellect, leading to a scientific and technological civilization where it in time will be possible to feed and support the growing populations of the world with a minimum of work, performed so that there will be ample time and energy for the realization of social, humanitarian, cultural, psychological, pedagogical, and esoteric projects. The only thing lacking is political will. This is suggested by Lucille Cedercrans with the words:

*"Remember that we have already arrived at that point where there is the beginning of the realization that each individual is an aggre-*

[1] Lucille Cedercrans: *Applied Wisdom – Volume II*, pp. 661 & 656.

*gate of consciousness which actually constitutes a group life... Your so called individuality is but an aggregate of a group; it is but a process, a process of the synthesis of the consciousness of the One Life in which you live, move and have your being.*[1] *After this identification has been attained to, and after you begin to realize what it means to identify as a Soul, then expand the upper half of your sphere to realize that just as you are an aggregate of the group consciousness below the surface of your appearance, or your presence, so are you a group consciousness above that surface; and simply identify then with the One Life".*[2]

At the same time, the esoteric teaching tells us that an age-old karmic problem, which has been holding back evolution for millions of years, has been solved by the victory over the "forces of resistance" in the 2 world wars – and especially the second.

When these aspects are considered together we may say that group consciousness is really just another step on the way to an all-embracing, planetary unitary consciousness which we esoterically know constitutes the structural basis of the system. This is expressed by the Tibetan in the following way:

*"From the hints given above it will be seen how the work of the Hierarchy in connection with mankind falls into two parts: – the work with individual human beings, in order to awaken them to soul consciousness, and then the work with them, as souls, so that (functioning then on soul levels and as conscious units in the kingdom of God) they can begin to vision the objective of God Himself. This second division of Their effort is only now becoming possible on a wide scale, as men begin to respond to the trend towards synthesis, and to react to the divine principle of coherence, so that (stimulated by their group relation) they can unitedly sense the vision and react to the principle of continuance. A hint is here given as to the true and future purpose of group meditation. More on this subject is not possible".*[3]

[1] Acts 17:28.
[2] Lucille Cedercrans: *Applied Wisdom –Volume II*, pp. 662 & 664.
[3] Alice A. Bailey: *Esoteric Psychology II*, pp. 240-241.

Somewhere else, the Tibetan goes deeper into the concept of group meditation and gives us one of the occult visions which makes the head spin for us ordinary people:

> *"For this the solar Angel,[1] the soul, is organising itself and re-orienting itself so that its power can be redirected into the world of men. Contact must be made by the soul between the lower aspect of its triple nature[2] and the aspect which has already found lodgment in the brain of man. Intelligent activity and love wisdom must be united, and the union must take place on the physical plane. In order to do this the soul is entering into "meditation deep", in union with all other souls who may have brought their instrument into a responsive state. This is the basic group meditation, and when a man achieves what the oriental books call "samadhi",[3] he has succeeded in participating, as a soul, in this group meditation, and enters upon that cycle of service which expresses itself through the planetary Hierarchy. The rational mind and the abstract mind function as a unit, and the motivating principle is love. The soul, expressing love and abstract intelligence, is at one with its expression on the physical plane through the brain, and, when this is the case, the lower man has synchronised his meditation with that of the soul".*[4]

## Group Consciousness

Many people are doubtful as to what exactly is meant by "group" and "group consciousness". Therefore, we will take a brief look at these concepts in a general sense.

A group is a state of consciousness which is distributed on several people. Their individual souls and the soul group bring them into incarnation together so that they may carry out a definite work which they are karmically connected to. Each group member incar-

[1] *Solar Angel*: The deva being who is putting substance at the disposal of the human principle of soul.

[2] The higher manas or abstract thinking of the soul.

[3] *Samadhi*: Corresponds to contemplation. From Sanskrit, *sam-âdha*, "self-possession".

[4] Alice A. Bailey: *A Treatise on White Magic*, p. 89.

nates in order to do a particular part of the work, and collectively they represent the project as a whole.

But how does the individual member become group-conscious? Group consciousness arises from an identification with the whole. Technically, we may say that it stems from atmic identification with the one life and buddhic experience of the unity of consciousness of humanity. It is this experience of synthesis and unity which is projected into the group life where it brings about group consciousness.

So, group consciousness is not something we develop by entering into or forming a group. It is a kind of consciousness which the individual person develops on his path of spiritual evolution, and which qualifies him to participate in group work.

If group consciousness was limited to the loving acceptance of the co-disciples in a group of people who work for a common purpose it would be as exclusive as love in the family life. It would keep others away from the community if they don't meet the requirements of that community.

Therefore, the most important function of an esoteric group is that the members meditate in order to build the "antahkarana", that is, the bridge from the physical brain to the higher self, for this is the only way to the experience of unity which is the basis of group consciousness. The soul in its own world is focused on the service work of the soul group, and the more the members of a physical group manifest the soul in its work the higher the level of group consciousness will be.

The love aspect of the group consciousness is contacted through aspiration, that is, dedication for the objectives and work of the group. It is this aspiration which attracts the objectives and the plan for their realization from the plane of the soul.

This shows us that real group consciousness isn't possible until a group includes a number of members with the 1st and preferably also the 2nd initiation. This does not mean that a group may only be formed by a group of people who are all initiates of the first degree. It means that the group should hold a sufficient number of people with initiation – the critical mass, as it is called today.

As the radiation of the group increases it cannot be avoided that the light also penetrates into the subconsciousness and stimulates the thoughtforms which represent personal obstacles to the work. Karmic patterns surface and meet with the clear consciousness of the group. Here it is important that these thoughtforms are seen from the plane of the soul and "transilluminated." Therefore, it is also important that the group has an instinctive understanding and accept of its hierarchical structure so that the influence of the initiated members becomes decisive in the treatment of the various forms of maya, glamour, and illusion which inevitably emerge in the group life.

Each group member should be aware of his karmic blockings and feel responsible for their dissolution in the loving atmosphere the group represents. The method is, as always, the joint raising of the consciousness into the light of the soul which transilluminates the "darkness" so that the person in question is free to serve. In this way, the group progresses despite the personality problems which will always be there. The group works as if these blockings are nonexistent – it raises above them.

This begins to happen when the group members are able to focus their consciousness in the heart centre. Then the problems are observed in an impersonal manner and ways of treating them appear. In some cases, a member has to postpone a clarification of the karmic problems until there is sufficient alignment of soul, mind, and brain, for the light of the soul is required if we want to illuminate a deep-seated problem and transform it.

As this happens to an individual group member it also happens to all the other members, for the progress of the group is not individual. All developments happen within the community that the magnetic field of the group creates. As time goes by the whole of the karmic situation is harmonized in the emotional field. At the same time, the mental body of the group is attuned to the intention and plan of the soul group and is gradually enabled to reflect the intentions of the Ashram in the physical world through its creative activity.

When the group consciousness has reached a sufficiently high level the group starts to attract people it can teach group work. Very often, these will appear to be "old friends", and there is nothing extraordinary about that because they are friends from earlier incarnations who become affiliated to the group in this way. At the same time, these people have the instinctive feeling that they can trust the members of the group.[1]

## Group Meditation

If a group of people wants to function on the above premises and realize the group ideals, their most important instrument is meditation. They simply use a common meditation as their individual morning meditation, and they use it in the same way. This means that if the meditation has a seed thought, all members of the group use the same seed thought for the same period of time. In this way, the work is synchronized, and on the mental plane a common field of tension is built, which is gradually growing in capacity and content.

The purpose of the group meditation is the same as the purpose of the individual meditation, namely, contact with the common soul principle of the group, which is emerging step by step as the service work and the joint meditation progress.

Through this soul principle, the group is gradually enabled to contact the Ashram, that is, the part of the Hierarchy the group is working for in particular, and today this affiliation is simplified considerably by the formation of the Ashram of Synthesis as the primary tool of expression of the Hierarchy in the realization of the plan of evolution. The Ashram of Synthesis holds all disciples on the 1st, 2nd, and 7th rays, and many of these are or will be in incarnation in our time, in order to participate in the work of manifesting human brotherhood in the physical world.

To support the work of group meditation it is wise to have a procedure for how the members may exchange their daily impressions from the meditation with each other. For, as the purpose of the whole project is to develop contact with the Ashram and contribute to the realization of its plans, an increasing accordance between the impressions of the group members will occur.

[1] See Lucille Cedercrans: *Applied Wisdom – Volume II*, pp. 656-709, Group Consciousness.

What really happens is that the group is gradually being "directed" by the Ashram so that eventually the two parts, the Ashram and the group on the physical plane, function as one mechanism of manifestation – something which is very characteristic of the influence of the 7$^{th}$ ray. In the beginning, these processes will be partly unconscious, and it is precisely here that an exchange of impressions between the group members may contribute to a gradually growing awareness of the situation.

Finally, when some of the group members have built the antahkarana or rainbow bridge to the soul or higher self, to such a degree that they are able to receive messages from the Ashram in their physical brain consciousness, the group enters the second phase of its work and can now with great efficiency help to realize the projects of the Ashram in the physical world, because its work rests on a directly understandable communication with the personnel of the Ashram. This is one of the primary methods of cooperation the Ashram will try to introduce in our time.

To write a group meditation is really relatively simple. We may take an individual meditation as our starting point, and then early in the meditation build in a few elements which will bring about the presence of the group members in the consciousness of the meditator. Once this presence is established it is the task of the individual member to sustain it during the rest of the meditation.

This may be difficult in the beginning, but as the work progresses and the group is building its own field of tension on the mental plane, it becomes easier and easier because the thoughtforms created during the meditation relate in a natural way to the group field. Eventually, the alignment of the individual member with the group during the morning meditation proceeds automatically, and, concurrently, every single individual contribution to the meditation work of the group will take part in the expansion and intensification of the common field of tension on the mental plane.

If we want to turn an individual meditation into a group meditation we may for instance introduce a visualization early in the meditation. We imagine that we sit in a circle with the other members of the meditation group. Then each member sends from his own heart a stream of golden love energy toward the heart of his neighbour to the right and sees how the stream flows about the whole circle, connecting heart with heart.

The efficiency of this procedure is emphasized by the words of the Tibetan:

> *"Only from the heart centre can stream, in reality, those lines of energy which link and bind together... This heart centre, when adequately radiatory and magnetic will relate you afresh to each other and to all the world... The activity of the heart centre never demonstrates in connection with individuals. This is a basic fact. What devastates most disciples is the solar plexus ability (when purified and consecrated) to identify itself with individuals. The heart centre cannot react, except under group impetus, group happiness or unhappiness, and other group relations".*[1]

After the visualization of the heart connection, the meditator says the mantra of group fusion in his mind:

> *"I am one with my group brothers, and all that I have is theirs.*
> *May the love which is in my soul pour forth to them.*
> *May the strength which is in me lift and aid them.*
> *May the thoughts which my soul creates reach and encourage them".*[2]

Now the presence of the group members in the meditation is established, and then it is merely a question of maintaining this state of consciousness the rest of the meditation. But in many cases, elements appear later in the meditation which are visualizations of how the group members perform a service work together.

But apart from synchronizing the morning meditation of the group members, it is also important that the members meditate together regularly. Here the full moon periods may be utilized, but naturally the group should see to it that this work does not interfere with the public full moon meditations[3] most esoteric groups organ-

[1] Alice A. Bailey: *Discipleship in the New Age II*, pp. 113-114.
[2] *Ibid.*, p. 245.
[3] Full moon meditation will be dealt with in the next section.

ize. These meditations are a very important part of the esoteric work of our time since they represent an opportunity for people who are not normally esotericists to participate in the work.

But let us see how a group meditation may be built. The meditation is read by one of the group members, and here it is important that the members take turns as it is difficult to read and meditate at the same time.

## Group Meditation

***Alignment***

Settle yourself comfortably, straighten the back, close your eyes, and relax your body. Take a deep breath, and then forget all about the breath. Raise your consciousness into the head...

Let us integrate the personality by saying 3 times OM – one time for each body. Imagine while you say OM that the body in question lights up and its activities are subdued...

*First the mental body ......... Say OM quietly and gently...*
*Then the emotional body ...... Say OM a little louder...*
*And finally, the physical body .. Say OM still louder...*

Raise your consciousness further up through the top of the head and connect it to the soul in the golden lotus above the head... Say a gentle OM which you "breathe" down through the top of the head. This establishes the soul-infused personality...

***Integration***

Now let us integrate the group. Send a stream of golden love energy from your own heart toward the heart of your neighbour to the right, and see how the stream flows about the whole circle, connecting heart with heart...

Say with me the mantra of group fusion:

> *I am one with my group brothers, and all that I have is theirs.*
> *May the love which is in my soul pour forth to them.*
> *May the strength which is in me lift and aid them.*
> *May the thoughts which my soul creates reach and encourage them.*

***Connection to Spiritual Centres***
Connect our group to the world-wide disciple group. See it as a golden lotus which serves as the heart centre of the New Group of World Servers.

Extend the connection to the Spiritual Hierarchy, the heart centre of the entire planet. Confirm this action by saying with me:

> *We assert the fact of our identification with Hierarchy, and we recognize that the divine will rules.*

See the Hierarchy as a gigantic golden lotus filled with white figures… Imagine that in the middle there is a golden triangle with the Masters M., D.K., and R. in the 3 points. This is the Ashram of Synthesis… In the centre, we see the Christ who is overshadowing the Ashram of Synthesis and is himself overshadowed by a greater triangle consisting of the Avatar of Synthesis, the Spirit of Peace, and the Buddha. See how the greater triangle draws the lesser triangle forth from the Hierarchy and connects with it point by point…

Extend the connection to Shamballa – the centre where the will and purpose of God is known… Imagine now that there is a pillar of light from Shamballa, through the Hierarchy and the disciple group down into our group…

*Meditation*
Let this image stay in the background of your consciousness while you hold your mind open to the impulses flowing down within the pillar of light. See how the 3 planetary centres – Shamballa, Hierarchy, and Humanity – gradually become integrated into one functioning whole. Then meditate on the seed thought of the month[1]... (5-10 minutes).

*Precipitation of Energies*
Imagine that a powerful impulse from the Christ – radiating the energies of the 2 triangles – flows down toward the earth in a spiral moving clockwise... See the impulse flow through the disciple group, the New Group of World Servers, our own group and out into the world through the 5 planetary inlets: New York, London, Geneva, Darjeeling, and Tokyo... Be also aware of the fact that humanity, itself, has invoked the impulse from the Christ, and that it forms a pathway of light for the descent of the Christ to earth...

Reflect on the impressions you have received and be ready to write them down after the meditation...

*Conclusion*
Say with me The Great Invocation, while you imagine that the light, love, and power of the group mingle with the impulse of the Christ and streams forth into world for the benefit of humanity and the other kingdoms in nature.

[1] Usually, there will be 12 seed thoughts changing every month during the year.

## Full Moon Meditation

Full moon meditation is a form of group meditation which is based on a few statements by the Tibetan Master, Djwhal Khul. Many esotericists today see him as the primary spokesman for the Spiritual Hierarchy, and he has, through his work with Alice A. Bailey, obtained a great influence on how the esoteric work is performed all over the world. He says:

> *"Occult students well know that at the time of the full moon certain high contacts are easier than at other times... At the time of the full moon (over a period of five days) the moon and the planet are the recipients of more reflected light from the sun than at any other time... Symbolically speaking, the period of intensest meditation of our planetary Logos comes around at the full moon period each month... This produces the pouring in of radiance and the entering in of energy both subjective and objective. For all true students, therefore, their work on the mental plane is facilitated; they are enabled then to meditate more successfully and to attain realisation with greater ease".*[1]

If we combine this statement with the next one we get a fairly good picture of the background for full moon meditations.

> *"The establishing of certain major festivals in relation to the moon, and in a lesser degree to the zodiac, will bring a strengthening of the spirit of invocation and the resultant inflow of responsive influences... The unified invocative thought of the masses and the focused, directed thought of the New Group of World Servers*[2] *constitute an outgoing stream of energy. This will reach telepathically those spiritual Beings Who are sensitive and responsive to such impacts. Their evoked response, sent out as spiritual energy, will in turn reach humanity, after having been stepped down into thought energy, and in*

[1] Alice A. Bailey: *Esoteric Healing*, pp. 340-341.

[2] *The New Group of World Servers*: A worldwide movement of people who have the good will and who consciously or unconsciously work with the preparations for the return of the Christ. It is a state of consciousness or an attitude, and not an organization.

*that form will make its due impact upon the minds of men, convincing them and carrying inspiration and revelation".*[1]

Together with other information, we get the picture that during 5 days about the full moon time each month – 2 days before, the day itself, and 2 days after – the Hierarchy turns the attention to humanity so that it becomes easier to have telepathic contact with the Masters and receive the ideas which are needed for the service work.

Nowadays, this service work is primarily focused on the preparations for the "Return of the Christ" as it is expressed with Christian nomenclature, or the "Externalization of the Hierarchy", as we say with esoteric terminology. Considerations of space forbid me to go into details with the event in this small book on meditation, but when it is mentioned at all it is because we are told that a new world religion is emerging in the life of our society, and that full moon meditations are really part of the sacramental aspect of this religion. They are simply the church services of our time.

As we have seen in the quotation above the Tibetan calls the periods "festivals". In this way, he emphasizes the eventfulness of the situations and makes them a little bit solemn.

The annual rhythm of the full moon times almost corresponds to the rhythm of the astrological signs, and therefore the full moon meditations are based on the signs of the Zodiac so that we can utilize the particular energies available in each sign. One way to do this is by using the keywords of the signs as seed thoughts in the meditations. These key words are:

Aries .... *I come forth and from the plane of mind, I rule.*
Taurus ... *I see and when the Eye is opened, all is light.*
Gemini .. *I recognize my other self and in the waning of that self, I grow and glow.*
Cancer ... *I build a lighted house and therein dwell.*
Leo ...... *I am That and That am I.*
Virgo .... *I am the mother and the child. I, God, I, matter am.*

[1] Alice A. Bailey: *The Externalisation of the Hierarchy*, pp. 419-420.

Libra ....... *I choose the way which leads between the two great lines of force.*
Scorpio ..... *Warrior I am and from the battle I emerge triumphant.*
Sagittarius ... *I see the goal. I reach that goal and then see another.*
Capricorn ... *Lost am I in light supernal, yet on that light I turn my back.*
Aquarius .... *Water of life am I, poured forth for thirsty men.*
Pisces ....... *I leave the Father's home and turning back, I save.*

Three of these full moon periods are particularly important: the full moon in the signs of Aries, Taurus, and Gemini. This is where the "spiritual" year ends and a new one begins:

- *Full Moon in Aries – The Festival of Easter.* This is the festival of the risen, living Christ, the Teacher of all men, and the Head of the Spiritual Hierarchy. Here the forces of restoration are particularly active. They are linked to the intelligence aspect and stimulates the human mind. They reorient the thinking of humanity and result in right human relations.
- *Full Moon in Taurus – The Wesak Festival.* This is the festival of the Buddha, the spiritual intermediary between the highest spiritual centre, Shamballa, and the Hierarchy. Here the forces of enlightenment are particularly active. They are linked to the love aspect and stimulate the intuitive understanding of people. They influence mass communication and media and bring about new educational systems.
- *Full Moon in Gemini – The Festival of Goodwill.* This will be the festival of the spirit of humanity, aspiring towards God, seeking conformity with the Will of God and dedicated to the expression of right human relations. It is also celebrated as the *World Invocation Day*. Here the forces of reconstruction are particularly active. They are linked to the will aspect and stimulate nations – not individuals. They stimulate the-will-to-synthesis in the UN and in time bring about world unity, peace, and plenty.[1]

[1] See Alice A. Bailey: *The Externalisation of the Hierarchy* and *The Reappearance of the Christ.*

In practical terms, the full moon meditation is held each month as close to the exact full moon time as possible. But as it is a public meeting it will usually take place in the evening so that people who go to work are able to participate. This means that the meditation is held the evening before the exact time, unless you are so lucky that the time coincides with the meeting.

As mentioned above, the period is really spread over 5 days. In the 2 days prior to the meditation, people prepare themselves by turning the attention to the coming event and concentrate on the particular qualities of the zodiacal sign. If we are part of an esoteric group we may together arrange which aspect of the service work we want to focus on, and then hope that the impressions the participants receive during the meditation relate to that aspect. We may easily imagine a situation where a part of the participants are merely present as individuals and profit by the fact that the arrangement is public, while another part is working concentrated from a plan which is conceived in advance.

On the day itself, it is wise first of all to be quiet – mentally. This is the best way of recharging the batteries for the event.

In the 2 days after the meditation, you concentrate on receiving, absorbing, and interpreting any impressions. Often, it is difficult for them to manifest in understandable form during the meditation itself because the level of energy may be very high and the consciousness has to adapt to the abstract and even symbolical impulses.

Full moon meditations may be done in many ways. Therefore, the following meditation is only an example of how it is done by one group – and at the same time, it is an indication of the fundamental elements which enter into its structure.

## Full Moon Meditation

***Alignment***

Sit comfortably, straighten the back, close your eyes, and relax your body. Take a deep breath, and then forget all about the breath. Raise your consciousness to the head…

Let us integrate the personality by saying 3 times OM – one time for each body. Imagine, while you say OM, that the body in question lights up and its activities are subdued…

First the physical body . . . . . . . . . . OM…
Then the emotional body . . . . . . . . OM…
And finally, the mental body . . . . . OM…

Raise your consciousness further up through the top of the head, and connect it with the soul in the golden lotus above the head… Say a gentle OM which you "breathe" down through the top of your head…

***Keynote***
Let us begin the meditation by giving the keynote for our work:

> *He who faces the light and stands within its radiance is blinded to the issues of the world of men; he passes on the lighted way to the great Centre of Absorption. But he who feels the urge to pass that way, yet loves his brother on the darkened path, revolves upon the pedestal of light and turns the other way. He faces towards the dark and then the seven points of light within himself transmit the outward streaming light, and lo! the face of those upon the darkened way receives that light. For them, the way is not so dark. Behind the warriors – twixt the light and dark – blazes the light of Hierarchy.*[1]

***Integration***
The next step is to integrate the group. Send a stream of golden love energy from your own heart toward the heart of your neighbour to the right, and see how the stream flows about the whole circle, connecting heart with heart…

[1] Alice A. Bailey: *Discipleship in the New Age II*, p. 15.

Say after me the mantra of group fusion:

*I am one with my group brothers, and all that I have is theirs.*
*May the love which is in my soul pour forth to them.*
*May the strength which is in me lift and aid them.*
*May the thoughts which my soul creates reach and encourage them.*[1]

***Connection to Spiritual Centers***
This month we are in the sign of... It is our intention during the meditation to be receptive to the energies of the sign, so that we may participate in uplifting and clarifying the consciousness of humanity...

Connect our group with the world-wide network of meditating disciple groups. See it symbolized by a golden lotus which serves as the heart centre of the New Group of World Servers...

Extend the connection to the Spiritual Hierarchy, the heart centre of the entire planet. Confirm this action by saying after me:

*We assert the fact of our identification with Hierarchy,*
*and we recognize that the divine will rules.*

See the Hierarchy as a gigantic golden lotus filled with white figures... Imagine that in the middle there is a golden triangle with the Masters M., D.K., and R. in the 3 points. This is the Ashram of Synthesis... In the centre, we see the Christ who is overshadowing the Ashram of Synthesis and is himself overshadowed by a greater triangle consisting of the Avatar of Synthesis, the Spirit of Peace, and the Buddha...

[1] Alice A. Bailey: *Discipleship in the New Age II*, p. 245.

Extend the connection to Shamballa – the centre where the will and purpose of God is known… Imagine that now there is a pillar of light from Shamballa, through the Hierarchy and the disciple group down into our group…

*Higher Interlude*
Let this image stay in the background of your consciousness, while you hold your mind open to the impulses flowing down within the pillar of light. See how the 3 planetary centres – Shamballa, Hierarchy, and Humanity – gradually become integrated into one functioning whole…

*Meditation*
Then meditate on the seed thought of the month[1]… (5-10 minutes).

*Precipitation*
Imagine that a powerful impulse from the Christ – radiating the energies of the 2 triangles – flows down toward the earth in a spiral which moves clockwise… See the impulse flow through the disciple group, the New Group of World Servers, our own group, and out into the world through the 5 planetary inlets: New York, London, Geneva, Darjeeling, and Tokyo… Be also aware of the fact that humanity itself has invoked the impulse from the Christ, and that it forms a pathway of light for the descent of the Christ to earth…

*Lower Interlude*
Imagine that our group now forms a centre of light in the great Ashram – the Ashram of Synthesis. See how the energy from the Christ shines on and illuminates the group as the light from the Sun. Say after me the mantra of the soul:

[1] The seed thoughts are the key words of the astrological signs which the full moon meditations are affilliated with – as they are indicated on pp. 94-95.

*In the centre of all Love I stand.*
*From that centre I, the soul, will outward move.*
*From that centre I, the one who serves, will work.*
*May the love of the divine Self be shed abroad*
*in my heart, through my group, and throughout the world.*[1]

***Distribution***

Say with me The Great Invocation while you imagine that the light, love, and power of the group mingle with the impulse of the Christ and streams forth into the world for the benefit of humanity and the other kingdoms in nature.[2]

[1] Alice A. Bailey: *The Externalisation of the Hierarchy*, p. 315.

[2] This meditation is closely related to the one formerly used by the World Service Intergroup, which was an international network of meditating disciple groups.

# Elements of Danger

We have now reached a point where we are in the possession of the necessary knowledge to begin meditating, and therefore it is also time to warn against certain elements of danger which are related to the process. This makes it possible for the student to be on guard against the form of enthusiasm – or perhaps we should say fanaticism – which will bring about harmful effects not only in the present incarnation, but also reflect themselves in several succeeding incarnations.

It is not the intention that we should disappear into the subjective realms and forget about the physical dimension, for this is where our service work and responsibilities lie, and the whole point of meditating is to give us a healthy balance between the 2 worlds so that the inner qualities may help us fulfill the outer obligations.

The best protection here is the common sense which tells us that progress in consciousness is a long-term project which isn't realized from day to day. This insight also compensates for the disappointment many beginners feel when great revelations do not appear as quickly as expected.

We have to realize that in relation to a subject like "meditation", which is really about manipulation of energy, essential information will always be kept back due to the dangers involved in imparting them. The "hidden" information usually deals with techniques which are effective precisely because they bring about marked effects rapidly and therefore are dangerous if they are used in a wrong way – technically, as well as in regard to motive.

For example, the primary goal of occult meditation is to teach a person how to transfer his consciousness from the lower to the higher self. This brings about the development of the ability to see on the causal plane, in the world of the soul, and intuitively perceive the personal conditions and weaknesses of other people. Naturally, this can only be allowed when the aspirant is able to be silent, unselfish, and stable. But how many people can fulfill these requirements? The responsibility is great and therefore caution is also great.

Usually, meditation is an activity a person starts on his own initiative – either as an individual effort or as a group work – but at some point it is necessary for everybody to come under expert guidance by a spiritual person, who has the qualities needed to supervise meditating people and protect them against the dangers which appear on the way.

Such a meditation teacher is rarely found in the outer physical life, if at all, though many meditation teachers claim that they meet these requirements. More often, it is the meditation process itself which leads a person to his teacher in the inner dimensions, and the teaching now takes the form of ideas and concepts which flow into the physical consciousness during or, in many cases, after meditation. These ideas are surrounded by a particular atmosphere which makes the meditator liable to trust them, and when he does, experience shows him that he is right in doing so.

So, it is not the intention that this section should discourage people from meditating but to make them follow the instructions they get and not deviate from them or insert foreign elements in order to obtain rapid effects. The effects will come, but it is not certain that they will come in this incarnation, and if this turns out to be the case, it simply shows that something is lacking in the preparational work, which, under any circumstances, must be done at some point – so why not now?

In the particular life, where the effects appear in the form of increased sensitivity, inspiration, and intuition, there will always be demanded physical "purity", emotional stability, and mental serenity before any further instructions are given. Not until the channel is really opened for intuition and closed for the instinctual nature is it wise to accelerate further. Not until the heart is wide open and the student feels a natural love for his fellow human beings can he move on. Not until the development is balanced and the intellect is not running ahead of the heart and keeping spiritual impulses out may he be entrusted with the qualities and abilities which, used in the wrong way, would have a devastating effect on his surroundings and himself. Not until he has no other life's purpose than serving humanity, the plan of evolution, and the Hierarchy can he be trusted with the formulas which bring the lesser devas under his control.[1]

[1] *Deva*: Invisible being who is a personification of the forces of nature.

But let us take a look at the various elements of danger which are related to meditation. Here are primarily 3 groups:[1]

1. Dangers inherent in the personality.
2. Dangers arising from karma and the surroundings.
3. Dangers connected with beings on the inner planes.

Often, these dangers arise in our "virtues" and not "vices", and that makes them difficult to handle. It may be a high-flying mental idealism which the lower self is quite unable to live up to. Aspiration, concentration, and determination are fine qualities, but if they are exaggerated they may lead to a destruction of the physical body which will block all progress for the rest of the incarnation. So, this is all about a sense of proportion which may be formulated in the following precautionary measures:

- Know yourself.
- Move forward slowly and with caution.
- Be aware of effects.
- Have the attitude that there is plenty of time, and that it is merely the personality who is in a hurry.
- Be regular and stable.
- Always remember that the real spiritual effects show themselves in the outer life of service.
- Also remember that psychic experiences are no sign of success.
- The surroundings will note the effects and assess them better than yourself.
- And above all, the Master is always informed, for the results will present themselves on the causal level long before you are aware of progress.

[1] See Alice A. Bailey: *Letters on Occult Meditation*, pp. 88-139.

## 1. Dangers Inherent in the Personality

They may be grouped under 3 headings: physical, emotional, and mental elements of danger.

*The Mental body*
This is the primary vehicle of the aspirant as it directs the 2 lower bodies. He tries to draw his consciousness from the physical and emotional body into the mental vehicle. Then he continues toward the causal body, using the antahkarana as a channel of communication. But under any circumstances, the mental body becomes his focus of consciousness, and here are 2 elements of danger:

1. *Blocking*. Some aspirants reach a point in their meditation where they with sheer will power block the processes of the mental body. They stop the natural circulation of thoughtforms, and this blocking affects the brain directly and is the cause of much fatigue. If the condition is allowed to continue it may lead to regular brain damage.
2. *Atrophy*. Some aspirants are so focused in the mental body that they run the risk of severing the connection to the 2 lower bodies. This creates atrophy in the lower bodies so that they no longer fulfil their purposes, and, as these bodies, among other things, are contributing to the growth of the causal body, this affects the entire evolutionary process. This reflects back on the mental body which becomes unproductive and very self-centered – an unrealistic dreamer whose dreams never materialize.

*The Emotional Body*
This is the most important body of the personality because it is the centre of consciousness for most people and the most difficult to control. This is due to the fact that the vibration of desire has dominated not only in the human kingdom but also in the animal and plant kingdoms, and that this activity therefore is age-old – contrary to the activity of the mental body. So, before the aspirant can enter the spiritual kingdom he has to eliminate the desire vibration and sublimate selfishness into spiritual aspiration.

During meditation, the emotional body has to be controlled by the will via the mental body. But this often leads to a negative – that is, receptive – condition, and if it is sustained too long it opens the door for obsession. So, the negative or receptive condition is not the goal. The emotional body must be positive or radiating in relation to the surroundings and everything which is lower, and only receptive to spiritual impulses coming from the causal body via the mind. Therefore, we have to be aware of:

1. The condition of the emotional body in regard to its positive-negative condition.
2. Its stability and conscious receptivity.
3. Its alignment with the mental and causal bodies. A defective alignment may cause the lower centers to become over-stimulated so that for instance sexuality is more difficult to control.
4. The possibility of obsession. The protection here lies in pure thoughts, spiritual goals, and unselfish service.

*The Physical Body*

Every human being incarnates with a physical-etheric body of a certain composition which is the result of earlier lives. It is now the task of the person to try to improve this body throughout the incarnation. The aspirant who begins meditating in the occult way is definitely playing with fire, for during the meditation he tries to contact the "solar fire" of the mental plane and the "electric fire" of the higher self.

If the meditation work is exaggerated before the alignment is stable the solar and electric fires may influence the latent kundalini fire[1] at the root centre and cause it to circulate too early. This results in disturbances and destructions instead of a vitalization and stimulation of the higher centers. This fire is supposed to follow a proper, geometrical spiral movement, depending on the soul ray of the aspirant and the vibratory frequency of his higher centers, and therefore it should not be allowed to circulate until the aspirant is able to direct it consciously according to verbal instructions from

[1] *Kundalini Fire*: Sanskrit, "serpent fire". The inherent energy of matter.

his teacher. Sometimes, the fire is awakened correctly without the aspirant knowing it in his physical brain consciousness. He knows it on the inner planes, but he has not succeeded in bringing this knowledge down into the brain.

Many of the dangers the physical body is exposed to originate in psychic functions and are outer manifestations of inner failings. Primarily 3 parts of the physical nature are exposed:

- The brain.
- The nervous system.
- The sexual organs.

*Dangers to the brain.* Here are primarily 2 forms:

1. *Congestion,* causing a suffusion of the blood vessels and a consequent strain upon the delicate brain tissue. This may lead to permanent damages and even imbecility. In the beginning, it shows itself as numbness and fatigue, but if the aspirant continues to meditate the results may be serious.
2. *Insanity,* which is often due to the fact that the aspirant is impatient and uses dangerous breathing exercises in order to arouse the kundalini fire. He pays the price of his impatience by losing his reason. The fire does not follow the correct geometrical shape, the necessary triangles are not formed, and the "electrical fluid" rushes with ever increasing speed and heat upwards, so that it literally burns away all or part of the brain tissue and in this way brings about insanity and sometimes death.

*Dangers to the nervous system.* These are far more common than those attacking the brain. Almost everybody who begins to meditate are aware of some effect on the nervous system. It may be insomnia, irritability, restlessness, or nervousness that does not permit any relaxation. All of this is unnecessary and may be avoided if the aspirant uses his common sense and doesn't accept abnormal states of consciousness in his eagerness to obtain results.

*Dangers to the sexual organs.* The primary danger here is overstimulation, as mentioned above. This is a very real danger, for in the case of over-stimulation the fire is merely following the path of least resistance due to the age-long polarization in that function. The remedy consists in withdrawing attention from these centers and turning the creative activity toward the mental plane. If the aspirant succeeds in doing so he transfers the activity of the fire to the throat centre. Therefore, it is apparent that unless a man is very advanced it is not wise to spend much time in meditation during the earlier years. This is the rule for the average person, but it is not so for disciples. They must solve their own individual problems.

## 2. Dangers Arising from Karma and Surroundings

The subject may be divided into 3 parts:

1. Personal karma in the present life.
2. National heredity and type of body.
3. Group affiliations, whether they are physical or exist on the inner planes.

*1.* Every human being incarnates with definite karmic tasks which are selected on the plane of the soul prior to incarnation. The danger is that meditation may prevent an aspirant from solving these assignments, so that he has to do it in a later incarnation. Let us assume that a soul has formed his 3 personality vehicles in such a way that the personality is able to develop the mental capacity necessary to perform scientific and technological work, and in this way expand the mental body for further use in future lives. At the same time, he may have in previous incarnations over-emphasized his heart aspect and spent several lives dreaming and seeing visions in the kind of meditation characteristic of mystics, and therefore he needs an incarnation in which he utilizes what he learns in the practical work on the physical plane. But still, he follows the path of least resistance and resumes his earlier tendencies, and the result is that he doesn't learn the lesson of that life but has to try again the next life and so on until the personality complies with the wishes of the soul. In this case, meditation is not a help but a hindrance.

2. Every type of human being is characterized by a definite emotional pattern. If we compare for instance an Italian with a German we are liable to express the difference in terms of emotional qualities such as burning, romantic, fluttering, phlegmatic, down-to-earth, sentimental, or similar expressions. It is therefore clear that these different temperaments have their own elements of danger, and that we by using a wrong meditation technique may over-stimulate a virtue into a vice, and the development of the causal body thereby becomes one-sided instead of the rounded balance the souls seeks. The goal of meditation is always the same, but meditation techniques vary according to the types of people who use them.

But naturally, if in the personality somewhere there is a real illness, hereditary fault, or mental weakness of some sort, it is not wise to meditate because the process may worsen the problem.

3. A thing which is often overlooked is the fact that when an aspirant becomes a probationer and begins to meditate his goal is not first of all to proceed with his own development but to qualify himself for serving his fellow human beings. If he neglects his immediate group relations, family, friends, acquaintances, or maybe an idealistic service group in order to develop certain capacities and qualities through persistent meditation, he runs the risk of crystallizing and succumbing to pride and arrogance and eventually taking the first step on the left-hand path. If his inner growth does not express itself in group service he treads a dangerous path. The same goes for the inner groups a disciple may belong to, such as the astral family, the "class" in the hall of knowledge, the group of invisible helpers, or mental groups such as the disciple group or soul group. In all these cases, a wrong meditation or a meditation performed in a wrong way may cause the disciple to offend against his group mates on outer or inner planes and in this way make mistakes he has to correct at a later occasion.

# 3. Dangers from Beings on the Inner Planes

The dangers consist primarily in obsession, and the obsessing entities may be divided into 3 groups.

1. Groups of discarnated humans on either the astral or mental plane.
2. Devas, either individual or in groups.
3. The dark brotherhood.

These dangers arise because of certain conditions in the bodies of the disciple which may very well be the result of meditation. For instance, it may be a trance-like and extremely negative (receptive) condition in all of the 3 personality bodies, as the result of a wrong meditation technique. This condition is like an open door to discarnated (deceased) humans who for some reason need to return to the physical plane.

It may also be a condition provoked by an ignorant and foolhardy use of certain sounds and mantras without the permission of the teacher. This connects the aspirant with certain groups of devas (nature forces) and makes him the target of their destructive influence.

And finally, it may be a very positive condition arising from the fact that the aspirant by means of meditation, in accordance with the occult laws and principles, and with the help of his teacher, starts to manipulate the "electric fluid" of the inner planes, and in this way attracts the attention of the dark brotherhood.

That this can happen at all is because most people in their inner bodies have a residue of substance which may respond to the vibration of the dark brothers, and therefore it is relatively easy for them to influence those bodies.

There are primarily 4 ways in which aspirants may protect themselves:

1. The recognition that purity in all bodies is a basic requirement. If a dark brother gets control of a disciple it merely demonstrates that he has a weakness of some sort. The door must be opened by the disciple himself.
2. Elimination of all fear. Fear creates a weakness, and weakness brings about dissolution. The weak point represents an opening where evil forces may enter.
3 Firmness and decisiveness no matter what happens. Your feet may be bathed in mud, but your head is bathed in sunshine. Recognition of the depravation of the earth does not necessarily lead to contamination.
4. The use of common sense. If we think through all situations thoroughly we will often find that what we experience is merely temporary and is in the nature of glamour and illusion. Sleep, relaxation, and amusement ensures that the body is never overworked.

# Conclusion

If we follow the human being back through history and further back through archaeology where it assumes the role of history, we clearly see that the human consciousness is evolving all the time. And it is not only cultural factors like natural science, technology, biology, and medicine which testify to this evolution. It is also other aspects of our civilization, such as systems of society, organization, administration, legislation, and all of the humanistic, psychological, sociological, and social dimension, which show us the immense difference between our modern form of life and the ones lead by earlier civilizations.

That our moral or ethical level may not have been able to keep in step with the other areas, and that war, hunger, and misery therefore still flourish widely, merely show that the evolution is far from completed. And still we have to admit that in some places on earth there is a reasonable degree or order, peace, and plenty which promise well for the future – even in the field of ethics.

This evolution of consciousness implies that we have been continuously expanding the perspective in which we see the world, so that today we may see it as a whole – a world woven together by radio, television, telephone, telegraph, and internet. We may even say that the human being is omnipresent, and we also realize that it is the mind which is the primary factor in this development.

Today, we understand many of the laws which govern the physical world, but we still lack the discovery and mapping of the laws of the spiritual dimensions. A few profound thinkers have been able to fathom these laws – figures like the Buddha, Pythagoras, Lao-tzu, the Christ, Plato, or Plotinus – and they have all sought to relate their experiences to posterity.

But because of the continuous evolution of consciousness there will come a time where many people – and not merely a few prominent individuals – will be able to have corresponding experiences and through them realize their higher spiritual potential. Then humanity as a whole will learn to regard the spiritual dimension as a fact in nature, and the science about its laws and principles will be part of the educational system which society offers its citizens.

It is here that meditation comes into the picture, for today there is a widespread interest for this activity many places on earth, and often we find that when a persistent tendency in one particular direction arises among people, it is the seed of the next step ahead in the human evolution of consciousness.

For meditation is a sort of intermediate link between the material and spiritual aspects of life. It enables consciousness to reach its true inner core – what we in Biblical terms call the "soul" – so that the human being may become the outer manifestation of its inner reality. This is the ultimate service a person may offer his surroundings – family, workplace, and society as a whole – for in the inner dimensions he gathers the impressions he needs for the development of his service work.

But to get that far demands a change of the entire way of life so that it includes 3 disciplines: meditation, study, and service. Meditation is the technique of development itself, study results in a profound philosophical view of life and gives at the same time the background for the development of the form which the meditation takes, while service is the practical consequence of the spiritual philosophy and makes sure that the knowledge the aspirant obtains is gained through experience and motivated by love of humanity.

At the same time, service functions as a high-pressure valve which leads excess energy out of the system before it makes any damage. A spiritual life will almost always entail a certain degree of over-stimulation because it is difficult for the aspirant to find the exact balance between inner stimulation and outer activity – the "golden mean" as it is called. And therefore, he will be liable to overdo the stimulation part just to be sure that something "spiritual" will happen.

Here it becomes very clear to us what limitations a book like this necessarily will have. They are closely related to the fact I have mentioned before in the book, namely, that, fundamentally, meditation is an aspect of the esoteric teaching and cannot really be studied or practiced independently of this teaching.

In the book, I have tried to limit the esoteric background material to an absolute minimum, but this has also meant that it is only the introductory phases of the meditation work which are touched upon. If we want to develop this work further and arrive at the final phases, which bring about the conscious union of personality and soul through the building of the antahkarana or rainbow bridge to the higher self, we have to study the esoteric teaching extensively.

This is partly due to the fact that the advanced form of meditation contains visualizations whose effect depends on a true perception of the inner mechanisms of consciousness. Occult meditation changes radically the whole of a man's being, including his physical and psychical organs of perception and awareness, that is, brain, nervous system, inner bodies, energy centres and many other things, which enter into that delicate, refined, and immensely intricate mechanism we call the human consciousness. And, as I have stated before, we cannot change something we don't know.

Let me give you an example. We are told that in the more advanced phases of human evolution spiritual progress depends on the ability of the disciple to direct the energies of his system through a network of triangles formed by the centres according to his ray structure. I think this makes it clear that knowledge of that kind requires a deep insight into the esoteric mysteries, which can never be obtained from publically available information but must come from within, through the development of states of awareness capable of intuitively apprehending such teaching. So, we are not talking about academic knowledge here, but knowledge gained through experience and motivated by love – in short, wisdom.

Now, to conclude, I would say that we can easily learn to meditate by the aid of this book – even if we don't have any esoteric knowledge at all – but if we consider meditation to be part of a more comprehensive spiritual program of development, which we would like to participate in, I will recommend that the reader seek education in the field or educate himself by extensive studies of esoteric literature. After the bibliography, I have appended a list of esoteric books for "beginners", which may be of help.

# The Great Invocation

*From the point of Light within the Mind of God*
*Let light stream forth into the minds of men.*
*Let Light descend on earth.*

*From the point of Love within the Heart of God*
*Let love stream forth into the hearts of men.*
*May Christ return to earth.*

*From the centre where the Will of God is known*
*Let purpose guide the little wills of men –*
*The purpose which the Masters know and serve.*

*From the center which we call the race of men*
*Let the Plan of Love and Light work out*
*And may it seal the door where evil dwells.*

*Let Light and Love and Power restore the Plan on earth.*

The above Invocation or Prayer does not belong to any person or group but to all Humanity. The beauty and the strength of this Invocation lies in its simplicity, and in its expression of certain central truths which all men, innately and normally, accept – the truth of the existence of a basic Intelligence to Whom we vaguely give the name of God; the truth that behind all outer seeming, the motivating power of the universe is Love; the truth that a great Individuality came to earth, called by Christians, the Christ, and embodied that love so that we could understand; the truth that both love and intelligence are effects of what is called the Will of God; and finally the self-evident truth that only through humanity itself can the Divine Plan work out.[1]

[1] May be found in all the works by Alice A. Bailey.

# Bibliography


Assagioli, Roberto: *Psychosynthesis*, Turnstone Press Limited 1986.

Assagioli, Roberto: *The Act of Will*, Turnstone Press Limited 1986.

Bailey, Alice A.: Discipleship, Initiation & Relationship with Masters, March 12, 1943, article from the website of The School for Esoteric Studies, www. esotericstudies.net

Bailey, Alice A.: *A Treatise on White Magic*, Lucis Press Ltd. 1951.

Bailey, Alice A.: *Discipleship in the New Age I*, Lucis Press Ltd. 1972.

Bailey, Alice A.: *Discipleship in the New Age II*, Lucis Press Ltd. 1955.

Bailey, Alice A.: *Esoteric Psychology II*, Lucis Press Ltd. 1970.

Bailey, Alice A.: *From Intellect to Intuition*, Lucis Press Ltd. 1960.

Bailey, Alice A.: *Letters on Occult Meditation*, Lucis Press Ltd. 1950.

Bailey, Alice A.: *The Externalisation of the Hierarchy*, Lucis Press Ltd. 1957.

Bailey, Alice A.: *The Light of the Soul*, Lucis Press Ltd. 1951.

Bailey, Alice A.: *The Reappearance of the Christ*, Lucis Press Ltd. 1948.

Cedercrans, Lucille: *Wesak*, Wisdom Impressions 2002.

Cedercrans, Lucille: *The Path of Initiation – Volume I-II*, Wisdom Impressions 2004.

Cedercrans, Lucille: *Applied Wisdom – Volume I-III*, Wisdom Impression 2007.

Cedercrans, Lucille: *The Nature of the Soul*, Second Edition, Wisdom Impressions 2011.

Cedercrans, Lucille: Meditation Defined, article, www.wisdomimpressions.com

Eastcott, Michal: *The Silent Path*, Rider 1989.

Linden, Jan van der: The Way of Meditation, article from the website of The School for Esoteric Studies, www. esotericstudies.net

Lucis Trust: Introductory Guide to Meditation, articles from the website www.lucistrust.org

Lucis Trust: The Science of Meditation, articles from the website www.lucistrust.org

Psychosynthesis Practice, Vol. 1, Psychosynthesis Exercises for Personal and Spiritual Growth. Compiled and edited by Thomas Yeomans, Ph.D. Psychosynthesis Distribution, California, USA.

# Esoteric Literature

## Suggestions for "beginners"

Bailey, Alice A.: Death: The Great Adventure, compilation. Lucis Press Ltd. 1985.
Bailey, Alice A.: *Initiation, Human and Solar,* Lucis Press Ltd. 1974.
Bailey, Alice A.: Ponder on This, compilation. Lucis Press Ltd. 1980.
Bailey, Alice A.: Serving Humanity, compilation. Lucis Press Ltd. 1977.
Bailey, Alice A.: *The Reappearance of the Christ,* Lucis Press Ltd. 1974.
Bailey, Alice A.: The Soul, compilation. Lucis Press Ltd. 1983.
Besant, Annie: *A Study in Consciousness,* Theosophical Publishing House 1980.
Besant, Annie: *A Study in Karma,* Theosophical Publishing House 1975.
Besant, Annie: *Avataras,* Theosophical Publishing Society 1900.
Besant, Annie: *Karma,* Theosophical Publishing House 1972.
Besant, Annie: *Reincarnation,* Theosophical Publishing House 1975.
Besant, Annie: *The Ancient Wisdom,* Theosophical Publishing House 1972.
Besant, Annie: *The Pedigree of Man,* Theosophical Publishing Society 1908.
Besant, Annie & C. W. Leadbeater: *Thought-Forms,* Theosophical Publishing House 1925.
Besant, Annie & C. W. Leadbeater: *Man: Whence, How and Whither,* The Theosophical Press 1947.
Cedercrans, Lucille: *The Soul and Its Instrument,* Wisdom Impressions 1995.
Cedercrans, Lucille: *Creative Thinking,* Wisdom Impressions 2001.
Cedercrans, Lucille: *Ashramic Projections,* Wisdom Impressions 2004.
Cedercrans, Lucille: *The Nature of the Soul,* Second Edition, Wisdom Impressions 2011.
Hodson, Geoffrey: *Basic Theosophy,* Theosophical Publishing House 1981.

Hodson, Geoffrey: *The Kingdom of the Gods*, Theosophical Publishing House 1952.
Hodson, Geoffrey: *The Light of the Sanctuary, The Occult Diary of Geoffrey Hodson*, The Theosophical Publishers Inc. 1988.
Leadbeater, C. W.: *Man Visible and Invisible*, Theosophical Publishing House 1964.
Leadbeater, C. W.: *The Astral Plane*, Theosophical Publishing House 1973.
Leadbeater, C. W.: *The Chakras*, Theosophical Publishing House 1973.
Leadbeater, C. W.: *The Devachanic Plane*, Theosophical Publishing House 1987.
Leadbeater, C. W.: *The Masters and the Path*, Theosophical Publishing House 1975.
Powell, Arthur E.: *The Astral Body*, Theosophical Publishing House 1972.
Powell, Arthur E.: *The Causal Body and The Ego*, Theosophical Publishing House 1972.
Powell, Arthur E.: *The Etheric Double*, Theosophical Publishing House 1969.
Powell, Arthur E.: *The Mental Body*, Theosophical Publishing House 1975.
Powell, Arthur E.: *The Solar System*, Theosophical Publishing House 1971.